P9-CCR-514

THE WAY TO PERFECT HEALTH

DAHNHAK

Seung-Heun Lee

Copyright 1999 by Seung-Heun Lee

Published by Dahn Publications

All rights reserved. No part of this
publication may be reproduced,
in any form or by means, electronic or
mechanical, including photocopying, recording,
or by any information storage and retrieval system,
without permission in writing from the publisher.

Dahn Publications

Dongil B/D 7F, 5, Soosong-Dong,

Chongro-Ku, Seoul 110-140, Korea

Tel: 82-2-722-7181, 91 Fax: 82-2-738-6167

ISBN 89-87293-05-X 13690

My body is not me, but is mine
Ki-energy brings health to the body and peace to the mind

THE WAY TO PERFECT HEALTH
DAHNHAK

Seung-Heun Lee

dahn

Thank You for the Devotional Support of
Suzanne Frazier
and Jerri Moss

TO CREATE
A HAPPIER AND HEALTHIER LIFE
FOR YOURSELF, YOUR COMMUNITY,
AND ALL OF HUMANKIND

CONTENTS

Preface ···13
Introduction ···19

PART I
WHAT IS DAHNHAK

1. The Definition of Dahnhak ···25
2. The Origin and History of Dahnhak ···26
3. The Purpose of Dahnhak Practice ···27

PART II
THEORY OF DAHNHAK

1. Dahnhak and Ki-energy ···31
2. The Dahn-Jon System: Integrative System of
   Energy Centers ···36
3. The Meridian System in the Body: Kyong-Rak and
   Kyong-Hyol ···40
4. The Three Principles of Dahnhak Practice ···46
5. Dahn-Jon Breathing: Meditative Breathwork ···55
6. Signs of Healing: Jin-Dong and Myong-Hyon ···61

PART Ⅲ
DAHNHAK PRACTICE

1. The Steps of Dahnhak Practice ···69
2. Practitioner's Memorandum ···72
3. Recommendations ···73
4. Basic Dahnhak Exercises ···74
   Do-In Exercise: Meridian Exercise ···74
   Ji-Gam Exercise: Ki-energy Awareness Exercise ···97
   Hang-Gong Exercise: Dahn-Jon Breathing Postures ···100
   Un-Ki-Shim-Gong: Conscious Control of
   Ki-energy ···110
   Dahn-Mu: Flowing with Ki-energy ···114
   Dahn-Gong: Advanced Level of Martial Arts ···126
5. Special Dahnhak Training Courses ···138
   Gae-Hyol: Meridian Channel Awakening ···138
   Shim-Sung: Developing a Relationship with the Self ···138
   Hwal-Gong: Therapeutic Exercise ···139
   Brain Respiration: Energizing and Rejuvenating the
   Brain ···139
   Taorobics: Combining Tao & Aerobics ···140

PART Ⅳ
SHARING

1. More than Recovering Health ···145
2. Finding My Soul and the Self ···148
3. Living in a World of Complete Harmony ···150
4. All My Stress Falls Away ···152
5. The Mind-Body Connection ···154
6. Newer and Deeper Meaning of Life ···156
7. True Happiness Inside Me ···158
8. In Harmony with Myself and the Universe ···160

Health Tips ···163
Where to Experience Dahnhak ···169
Glossary ···173
Index ···181
About the Author ···185

PREFACE

How to Create a Healthier Society and a Healthier Culture

People are beginning to wake up to the fact that the foundation upon which civilization has been built is not as stable as first imagined. There are no guarantees that life on this planet will continue. The human race has reached the point where a choice must be made. Either we choose to end life on Earth through destructive behaviors towards ourselves, each other and the planet, or we begin anew in the next millennium.

The choices made in the next few years will determine the future of the planet. These decisions can either be made from a limited collective wisdom or from an expanded understanding. This is a time of great challenges. It is a time of testing the potentialities and abilities of the human race.

Throughout history, attempts have been made to integrate the world into a unified whole. Religion and ideology have been used to create consensus between conflicting regions of the world. When religion or ideology were not successful, however, leaders used war and force in an attempt to unify the world. The common thread throughout all of these attempts at unity resulted not in harmony but in continued hostility between the winners and losers of the conflicts.

The solution to the present global problems will not be achieved through religious faith, moralistic instruction, intellectual scrutiny or scientific examination. The answers must arise out of universal values which all human beings hold as truth. Collectively, the human race must "experientially feel," instead of "intellectually understanding," what is known to be true.

Survival on this planet is dependent upon the truth that "our neighbors are the same as ourselves." All living things are interconnected. All of humanity can experience what Jesus, the Buddha, and Krishna taught. When this happens, people will begin living their lives, not individually but collectively, in a way that is called "enlightened."

Enlightenment or spiritual self-completion is no longer a personal achievement. This growth in human consciousness must become a massive social movement, a universal life-style, and eventually a global culture. When this happens, the human race will be able to deal with pressing issues from a unified, global perspective.

These ideas are not dreams. Enlightenment for the human race is possible right now. There is a way to build an "enlightened culture" by reawakening the senses and rediscovering the inner light. Conflicts can dissolve. Relationships can improve. Consciousness can arise. The human race can move past the present global struggles for survival into a new way of living on Earth. This is not an intellectual movement. This is a movement based on the spontaneous awareness of people.

The Dahnhak program began when people joined me every morning in a public park in a small town in South Korea to practice breathing exercises. Through these exercises, the practitioners regained their health. From this simple beginning in 1983, Dahnhak has gained momentum.

It has grown into a global undertaking challenging the people of the world to make a transformative cultural shift.

The Dahnhak Practice is based simply on "breath." All living beings breathe. Even though breathing is necessary for survival on this planet, it is taken for granted by most people. Few people pay attention to their breathing, but the quality of the breath has great implications on health and consciousness.

Breath can be either controlled autonomously by the body or intentionally by the mind. Whether people pay attention to their breath or not, they continue to inhale and exhale.

Breath also dramatically demonstrates the interconnectedness between people. The air and energy that one person breathes in are the same air and energy other people have just breathed in and out. Becoming aware that everyone shares the same air is the beginning of understanding that all living things are interconnected on many levels.

Most people think of themselves as separate. With each conscious breath, they can draw closer to understanding that existence and identity arise out of a source of life that is not within the body. They begin to understand intuitively that existence is not confined inside the body or within a limited lifetime. Awareness begins to arise of the Ultimate Oneness between heaven, earth, and human beings. With this recognition, they begin to see themselves from a limitless open holistic perspective instead of the past restrictive posture. This is the beginning of Cosmic Consciousness.

Since 1985, when the first Dahn Center was established, increasing numbers of people have experienced the Dahnhak Practice. Today, more than 100,000 people are participating at 360 Centers throughout the world. In addition, a number of people are enjoying the daily Dahnhak Practice held in 2,000 public parks throughout South Korea.

Within the Dahnhak Practice, there is a pattern of development which most practitioners experience. Many people begin to practice Dahnhak with the intention of improving their own health. After some time, their attention moves from the health improvement to mental and spiritual concerns. As they transform themselves into well-rounded, harmonious, caring individuals, they expand their participation into other areas of social or public activity.

After watching this particular development pattern appear naturally in so many practitioners, it became obvious that Dahnhak is more than an exercise program to improve health. It is a holistic social education system. Practitioners willingly volunteer to share their own experience of discovering their mind/body health with others who are seeking what they had been seeking when they found the Dahnhak Practice. Students become teachers. Over 10,000 students are now Dahnhak teachers throughout the world.

Dahnhak teachers have a tendency to do more than the average citizen does. They want to serve wherever they can. Wherever they are, they naturally and easily share their experiences from the Dahnhak Practice. Since the breathing exercises are so easy to teach, Dahnhak teachers can inspire future students at any time.

These teachers are like water. They give life to what they serve. They are flexible and unpretentious. No two teachers are alike. Wherever they are, like water, they make everything grow into its full potential. They permeate into the uncared-for corners of the society to irrigate and fertilize the life around them. They are humble and unobtrusive.

Their good works are often times so spontaneous that they are unaware of the beneficial results.

Their life-style is so natural that other people want to copy it. Effortlessly and spontaneously, a new culture is being created which is more responsible, more considerate, more accepting, more enlightened. It is a testimony to human consciousness moving out of adolescent behavior into a wisdom encompassing the power to direct all action towards creative and peaceful purposes.

In the present civilization that discourages enlightened life-styles, I hope Dahnhak will be a breath of fresh air inviting humanity to join in the restructuring of the culture. Inviting people to move towards the truth of their personal existence and the understanding of the interdependence of all living beings is bringing about a new global perspective.

By Seung-Heun Lee
From Sedona, Arizona
March, 1999

INTRODUCTION

By Dinohra M. Munoz-Silva, M. D.*

I was introduced to Dahnhak by accident. As a psychiatrist, I quickly recognized that this was not just an exercise program. It is a process that benefits your entire being.

Having practiced traditional Hatha-Yoga, I was aware that exercise could be used to relax the mind and stimulate the body. Since experiencing the Dahnhak Practice, I have expanded my opinion. With this exercise, you can also heighten your sense of awareness. You can genuinely awaken your sense of being and unify the mind, body and spirit.

An important component of the Dahnhak exercise is learning to listen to your inner Self and following your instincts. Through this remarkable program, you can become one with your body, mind and spirit. You can expand the limits of yourself beyond your present belief system. With this practice, your potential is unlimited.

Through the Dahnhak Practice, you can discover a state of harmony with others in an environment that supports acceptance, tolerance and patience. You will uncover your strengths as well as your weaknesses in your personal search for the truth. You will begin to take responsibility for your actions with a willingness and desire to change habits that are not useful.

This form of exercise is gradual yet gentle. Everyone in the program moves along at his/her own pace and level of comfort. Among the practitioners, there is no competition or rivalry; just a sense of unity and a heartfelt responses.

The Dahnhak Practice has 3 components: (1) Physical exercise; (2) Accessing Ki-energy through visualization and imagery; and (3) Meditation. By the end of each session, you will have integrated all three aspects of the practice. As you proceed through the program, you will move through different levels of physical exercise, accessing Ki-energy and meditation. The goal of each step is to help you achieve a level of consciousness where your true identity manifests itself.

This is an enriching experience, irrespective of age, physical ability or meditation experience. The results of this practice are a sense of peace and harmony. As you proceed through the exercises, the limits of your abilities will be expanded beyond your present imagination.

Today, people are caught up in their lives and there is little time for any type of exercise program. Within the Dahnhak Practice, you will feel a sense of calm that will provide the underpinning of peace with which you will be able to handle your fast-paced, demanding life-style. After a while, practitioners find that they stop becoming involved in antagonistic circumstances that are filled with conflict and turmoil. Instead, they turn to healthier and more positive ways to interact with their family, friends and business associates.

They find that their relationships become more stable

and mature. As they begin to feel the Ki-energy flow in their bodies, they learn how to respect their own bodies. As their feelings of separateness begin to dissipate within the Dahnhak exercise group, they discover that the energies in the practice hall become one, filling the room with happiness, joy and peace. Their fears and apprehensions disappear in an atmosphere of love and acceptance.

At this point, the practitioners understand what it is like to have a desire to achieve excellence in their lives and their relationships. Their lives begin to change. They take on a holistic approach to life, with a sense of well-being, happiness, joy and harmony.

Through Dahnhak, you are asked to follow your own true vision. You are encouraged to find your True Self. It is now time for you to start on a journey you are entitled to experience. Feel the force of your energy and enjoy the experience of the Dahnhak Practice.

* Dr. Munoz-Silva is a certified psychiatrist with over fifteen years of clinical experience in academic medicine and private practice in the New York City area and the mother of four beautiful children.

Awakening

It was a still, starry night.
One shining star suddenly came into me
and whispered.
It is your eyes that are watching the stars
shining over there,
and it is your ears, not you,
that hear the raindrops
flowing down the window.
I used to think I was watching the stars
and I was hearing the raindrops.
Now I see once more with awakened eyes
and I hear once again with opened ears,
to realize I am the shining star,
and I am the raindrop.
The bright star sparkled once again
to show me that I am
neither the shining star nor the raindrop.
I found out who I am and everything became clear.
Words fail to say the unspeakable and indescribable.
Stars are still shining on the sky through the window
and raindrops are still falling in the same way.

Seung-Heun Lee

PART I

WHAT IS DAHNHAK

1. The Definition of Dahnhak

Dahnhak is a holistic health program that teaches people how to utilize Ki-energy. "Dahn" means "energy, vitality, and origin of life," and "hak" means "study, philosophy and theory."

This program supports healthy ways of living and encourages the desire to seek Human Perfection. The philosophy of Dahnhak is based on the belief that human perfectibility is attainable, irrespective of sex, age or race. The Dahnhak program gives people an integrated method to discover for themselves their relationship to their body, their mind, and finally to ultimate reality, their "True Self."

2. The Origin and History of Dahnhak

The roots of the Dahnhak Practice extend several thousand years back into Korean history. It began as an ancient Korean training program to educate the population on how to develop both mind and body. It was practiced on a daily basis with the intent of maintaining health and developing potential power to become ideal humans. During those times, it was a common knowledge that individual well-being was an illusion. The knowledge that no living thing can exist even for a moment without the cooperation of other living beings was understood from experience. Dahnhak contributed to the mental and physical well-being and political unity of the Korean people.

Up until two thousand years ago, this educational method was practiced and transmitted by wise men to each generation. However, the Korean people failed to keep the Dahnhak tradition alive.

The Dahnhak tradition was rediscovered by Seung-Heun Lee through his own journey into self-realization and rigorous self-discipline. He took the traditional system and modernized it. He began teaching Dahnhak at the public parks in South Korea to anyone who was interested in the exercises.

In 1985, Seung-Heun Lee opened the first Dahn Center in Seoul. Since that time, the program has expanded throughout the world with 360 Centers offering Dahnhak training to over 100,000 people. The tradition of offering the exercises continues in 2,000 public parks in Korea and overseas.

3. The Purpose of Dahnhak Practice

The purpose of Dahnhak is to give individuals the opportunity to realize their own personal power. Through experiencing Ki-energy, the true source of life, they discover how Ki-energy works in their bodies and how they can utilize it for optimal health.

During Dahnhak Practice, practitioners learn to communicate with their bodies. They discover that they can become the real masters of their bodies with the ability to control and regulate their bodily functions. By stimulating the Ki-energy circulation, the body's natural healing power is activated. When their bodies are recharged with fresh Ki-energy, the practitioners can lead themselves back to optimum health, naturally healing most physical and mental diseases.

When practitioners arrive at their goal of a healthy life, they usually extend their intentions towards creating harmonious relationships with their family, friends, acquaintances and nature. This new holistically healthy life style by practitioners contributes to leading the rest of the world into a new culture supporting happier and healthier human beings.

Joy of Finding Self

How happy I feel on the way to my Self!
I'm on the happy road to find the Self.
If you go astray leaving the Self,
You will have aching feet
before going Ten Miles.

What a joy I'm having on the way to my Spirit!
I'm on the happy road to meet the Spirit.
If you go astray leaving the Spirit,
You will have aching feet before
reaching the Tenth Village.

I am happy on the way to Our Self.
I'm on the happy road to join Our Self.
If you go astray leaving Our Self in yourself,
Your aching feet will fail you
far away from the City of Ten.*

A Korean Folk Song

* The word "Ten" in Korean means perfection and enlightenment.

PART II

THEORY OF DAHNHAK

1. Dahnhak and Ki-energy

"Ki" is the Korean word for cosmic vitality that is the true essence of every creation in the cosmos. Most people begin their understanding of Ki by experiencing it as bio-energy or the vital life force in the body. Ki is the connection between the physical body and conscious mind. When practitioners learn to control the Ki in their bodies, they begin to understand that they have control over their bodies. In the Orient, people have known about Ki for thousands of years. Oriental medicine, such as acupuncture or acupressure, utilizes the knowledge of Ki-energy by healing people through correcting the distorted energy flow in their body.

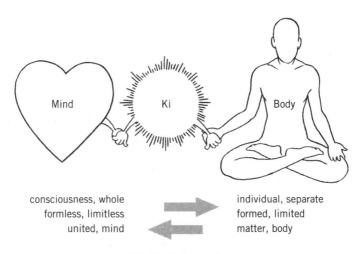

consciousness, whole	individual, separate
formless, limitless	formed, limited
united, mind	matter, body

**Mind/Body Connection
through Mediation of Ki-energy**

Ki-energy: Cosmic Energy

Ki-energy is another name for cosmic energy. It is the energy that circulates throughout the universe. As the poets have written, all human beings are made up of stardust and cosmic energy. This is the connecting thread that helps human beings understand that all beings in the cosmos exist as one. As many religious and spiritual traditions have tried to impart, all living beings residing on earth are individual components of the Oneness of the universal Ki-energy. The concept of Oneness changes for practitioners from an intellectual concept to one of knowing, through actual experience, that Ki-energy moves throughout the body.

It is overwhelming for human beings to imagine the immense power of the energy circulating through the vast universe. When people are connected with that universal energy, the Ki-energy in their bodies actively circulates like the movement of the solar system.

To connect and interact with this energy is very easy: breathe. Everyone inhales and exhales whether or not they are conscious of this activity. Through the Dahnhak breathing exercises, practitioners become aware of inhaling as the taking in of universal Ki-energy and exhaling as the releasing of used, dissipated energy back into the universe. This energy-focused respiration is called "Dahn-Jon Breathing."

Three Types of Ki-energy: Won-Ki, Jong-Ki and Jin-Ki

Knowledge of Ki-energy is extremely beneficial prior to beginning the Dahn-Jon Breathing exercises. Ki-energy flows through the human body in three different ways:

Won-Ki, Jong-Ki and Jin-Ki. "Won" means "innate," "Jong" means "stamina or strength," and "Jin" means "true or genuine."

1) **Won-Ki**: The first type of Ki-energy is inherited energy. Human beings receive this energy at birth from their parents.

2) **Jong-Ki**: The second type of Ki-energy is acquired energy from nourishment. This energy source is replenished through diet and respiration.

3) **Jin-Ki**: The third type of Ki-energy is received through pure cosmic awareness and is accessible through relaxed concentration.

Jin-Ki: The Essence of All Energy

Jin-Ki is accessed through deep mindful concentration of the breath. Upon inhalation of breath, Jin-Ki, pure cosmic energy, enters the body. It is the power of the mental concentration which invites the cosmic energy to circulate throughout the body as Jin-Ki. Since Jin-Ki is an energy which is accessed by the concentration, it can be controlled by a person's will power. The following exercise demonstrates how will power can control Jin-Ki.

Place your concentration in the center of your palm. Concentrate on making that part of your palm warmer than the rest of your hand. After a while, compare the temperature in the center of your palm to another part of your body. The heat in your palm is the collection of the Jin-Ki, placed there by your will power. Wherever in the body that you focus, that is where the Jin-Ki goes.

The strength and quality of the Jin-Ki is dependent on a person's quality of consciousness, ability to concentrate and stability of emotions. Love, peace, hatred, jealousy, anger, possessiveness, greed, selfishness, or pride influences the type of energy accessible to the body. Positive ideas and emotions create positive energy, permitting the Jin-Ki to flow easily throughout the body. Negative emotions and ideas reduce the effectiveness of the flow of Jin-Ki. It becomes contaminated, heavy, and stagnant. Blockages in the flow of the Jin-Ki cause disease and unbalance in the body.

Breath: Access of Ki-energy

For most people, it is common for their minds to jump from one idea to the next. They believe that they have no control over what they think or how they feel. They have given up the power to control their mind. To create positive energy, they have to have positive ideas and positive emotions. That means they have to be able to control their minds and make them think positively. Taking back the control of the mind and its thoughts is very simple. The key is the breath. Learning to take control of the breath enables practitioners to control their mind and themselves. When this happens, they are able to become masters of themselves.

Every breath carries the same inhalation of life and exhalation of death. But the breath carries something more than life or death. It contains something in-between and beyond these concepts. Breath is natural, simple, easy, universal and priceless. To begin to understand the breath, a person must experience the breath as both autonomous and controllable. Since the breath is connected to both the autonomous system and the conscious mind, it is the bridge between the body and mind. With practice, the breath becomes the gateway to deeper layers of consciousness. Concentrating on inhalation and exhalation permits the Jin-Ki to enter the body and with that comes the realization that there is an invisible connection between the body and universe.

2. The Dahn-Jon System: Integrative System of Energy Centers

The acupressure points, which are part of the organic energy system of the body, work synergistically to create the larger energy center called Dahn-Jon. "Dahn" means "Ki-energy." It also means "red." "Jon" means "field or center." In Dahnhak Practice, seven Dahn-Jon energy centers are identified in the body. These energy centers are not organs. They exist in the body on an energetic level not a physical level. They are located in areas where several acupressure points are in close proximity to each other. They form a cooperative system which controls the activities of the bodily functions through accumulating and synthesizing the vital Ki-energy.

Dahn-Jon is shaped like an egg or a ball. Sometimes, the Dahn-Jon is described by practitioners as like the sun. As Ki-energy collects inside the Dahn-Jon, it may grow

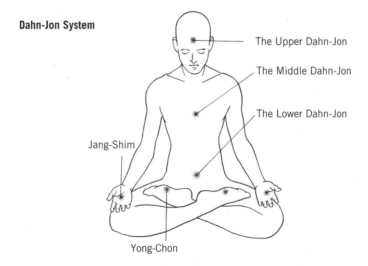

Dahn-Jon System

The Upper Dahn-Jon

The Middle Dahn-Jon

The Lower Dahn-Jon

Jang-Shim

Yong-Chon

from the size of a chestnut into something larger than a basketball. Practitioners feel their Dahn-Jons differently, according to their sensitivity to Ki-energy and the degree of their activation of the energy centers.

There are seven Dahn-Jons in the body:

Three Internal Dahn-Jons: Lower Dahn-Jon
Middle Dahn-Jon
Upper Dahn-Jon
Four External Dahn-Jons: 2 Jang-Shim
2 Yong-Chon

In the Dahn-Jon System, if one or more of the seven energy centers are blocked, the Ki-energy flow in the body is reduced and the interchange of Ki-energy with the cosmos weakens, causing disease. As the Dahn-Jon System becomes unblocked through Dahnhak Practice, the flow of the Ki-energy is restored, improving physical health and a feeling of peace.

Three Internal Dahn-Jons

All three of the Internal Dahn-Jons are unique in their function. Lower Dahn-Jon is located two inches below the navel and two inches inside the abdomen. The function of this energy center is to accumulate the vital Ki-energy and circulate the energy throughout the entire body. The color of the energy of Lower Dahn-Jon is red. When the Lower Dahn-Jon becomes fully developed, the body becomes filled with fresh vital energy and physical strength is increased. During the exercises, when references are made to the Dahn-Jon, it usually means the Lower Dahn-Jon.

Middle Dahn-Jon is located around the Jon-Jung, an acupressure point between the breasts. This is the place of human emotional energy, characterized by unconditional love. When the Middle Dahn-Jon is activated, practitioners feel a state of mind that is peaceful and tranquil. They have the capacity to direct unconditional love towards others.

When a person begins to feel the Ki-energy in the Middle Dahn-Jon, their communication of feelings and interaction with others improve to a level of complete understanding. Emotion is energy. When people feel stressful from strong negative emotions, the Middle Dahn-Jon will become blocked with impure energy. When the Middle Dahn-Jon becomes blocked, the energy circulation is reversed. This condition leads to many diseases of the nervous or circulatory system. The color of the energy of the Middle Dahn-Jon is gold.

Upper Dahn-Jon is located near the In-Dang, an acupressure point between the eyebrows. It is activated by pure energy. The color associated with the Upper Dahn-Jon is indigo. When the Upper Dahn-Jon becomes activated, practitioners experience clear awareness.

The activation of the Upper Dahn-Jon is the key to unfolding the higher abilities of the human brain. As the brain wave lowers into an alpha state, consciousness becomes one with cosmic energy. Personal identity is lost and is replaced by an understanding of Cosmic Consciousness. This is when the practitioner awakens into a new dimension of mind.

Four External Dahn-Jons

Two of the four External Dahn-Jons are located in the palms of the hands called Jang-Shim. The other two External Dahn-Jons are located in the soles of the feet, called Yong-Chon. They are the main channels for energy interchange between the human body and the cosmos. They function as gates supplying the body with Ki-energy from the huge reservoir of cosmic vitality.

3. The Meridian System in the Body: Kyong-Rak and Kyong-Hyol

Ki-energy moves through the body along pathways called Kyong-Rak or meridian channels, like the body's circulatory system which flows through veins and arteries. On meridian channels, there are specific points called Kyong-Hyol or acupressure points. The acupressure points are like holes through which Ki-energy enters and exits the body with the breath. Upon inhalation, the flow of the Ki-energy enters the body at the acupressure points and moves through the meridians to the vital organs of the body.

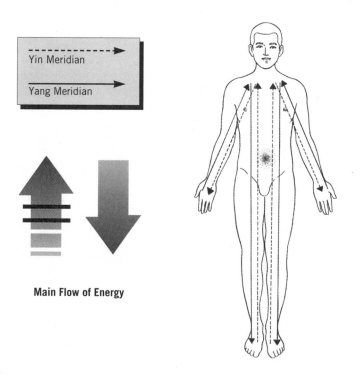

Yin Meridian

Yang Meridian

Main Flow of Energy

There are 12 meridian channels, 365 acupressure points in the human body. The major acupressure points are listed below:

1) **Bak-Hoe**: At the crown, top of the head, where many important meridian channels meet at one point. In newborn babies, this point is open and the hard shell of the skull has not covered it over. In the Dahnhak Practice, when practitioners become aware of their sixth sense, this is the point through which the celestial energy is received into the body. This point is also called the Great Gate to Heaven.

2) **In-Dang**: Between the eyebrows. Once this acupressure point is open and functional, clairvoyant power is available to the participant to see into all manner of things. This point is called "the eye of Heaven" or "the Third Eye."

3) **Jon-Jung**: Between the breasts.

4) **Ki-Hae**: Two inches below the navel. Ki-Hae means "the

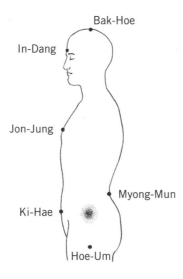

sea of Ki-energy." The Lower Dahn-Jon is located about two inches inside the body from the Ki-Hae.

5) Hoe-Um: The perineum.

6) Myong-Mun: On the back directly opposite the navel, between the 2nd and 3rd lumber vertebrae. "Myong-Mun" means "the gate of life." Cosmic vital energy enters the body through this point during Dahn-Jon Breathing exercise.

7) Jang-Shim: At the center of the palm on each hand. The location is determined by making a fist, and where the middle finger touches the palm. As an External Dahn-Jon energy center, it is a sensitive acupressure point.

8) Yong-Chon: On the sole of foot, approximately in the center, just below the ball of the foot. Yong-Chon is an External Dahn-Jon energy center.

Jang-Shim   Yong-Chon

9) Jok-Sam-Ri: On the outside of the leg, just below the knee, and in between where the two leg bones meet.

10) Tae-Chung: On the top of each foot, at the point where the bone of the big toe and the second toe join, between the first and second metatarsal.

Jok-Sam-Ri   Tae-Chung

To wake up the entire meridian system throughout the body, Dahnhak Practice has an exercise called "Body Patting." It is an easy and effective way to stimulate all the acupressure points along the meridian system to encourage the Ki-energy to move throughout the body. Every cell of the body will be stimulated and refreshed by the circulation of Ki-energy. This exercise will also remove any stagnant or blocked energy along the meridian system.

1) Stand with legs shoulder width apart.
2) Begin by patting the chest with both hands. Move back and forth across the chest, stimulating all the acupressure points on the upper chest. Increase the

strength of the patting until it almost becomes a slapping movement.

3) Raise the left arm with palm facing up. Pat with the
right hand from the left shoulder, down the inside of
the left arm, inside of the elbow, wrist, palm and fingertips.

4) Clap hands ten times.

5) Then, turn the left arm over so that the palm is facing
down. Begin patting the back of the left hand, up the
back of the wrist, the outside of the arm, the outside of
the elbow, back up to the left shoulder.

6) Continue patting across the chest.

7) Repeat the same patting motion for the right arm.

8) Continue patting while moving both hands back to
the middle of the chest. Move the hands to the stomach and liver and keep patting.

9) Move the hands to the abdomen and pat the Dahn-
Jon 100 times.

10) Next, bend over slightly and pat the area of the back
where the kidneys are located. Pat gently, stimulating
the kidneys but not jarring them.

11) Continue patting while moving to the hips.

12) Continue patting and move down the outside of the
legs, the thighs, knees, ankles, and the top of the feet.

13) Pat going up along the inside of legs and raise your
upper body.

14) Finally, return the hands to the abdomen and gently
pat Dahn-Jon. Rub the abdomen in a clockwise direction. Then, gently sweep the body from the top of the
shoulders to the feet.

4. The Three Principles of Dahnhak Practice

There are three principles upon which Dahnhak Practice is based:

1) **Su-Seung-Hwa-Kang**: Water Energy Up, Fire Energy Down
2) **Jong-Chung, Ki-Jang, Shin-Myong**: Health to Enlightenment
3) **Shim-Ki-Hyol-Jong**: From Mind to Matter

Su-Seung-Hwa-Kang: Water Energy Up, Fire Energy Down

There are two kinds of energy in the body: warm fire energy and cold water energy. When the body is in balance and optimum health is achieved, the water energy is located in the head and the fire energy is maintained in the abdomen. This state is called "Su-Seung-Hwa-Kang." "Su" means "water," "Seung" means "go up," "Hwa" means "fire," and "Kang" means "come down." "Su-Seung-Hwa-Kang" expresses the universal principle that water energy must go up and fire energy must come down. This is first of the three principles of the Dahnhak Practice.

There are examples, in nature, of water moving up and fire moving down such as the circulation of water throughout the planet. In the ocean, the radiant heat (fire) comes down from the sun and evaporates the water, creating vapor that rises up to form clouds. The rain falls back to earth. This system of "fire down" and "water up" creates the endless circulation of moisture throughout the planet.

Another example from nature is the process of photo-synthesis in plants. Every plant receives "fire energy" coming down from the sun. The plant's roots pull up the "water energy" from the earth. With the combination of "fire down" and "water up," the plant processes the sunlight and water to flower and bear fruit. When they lose the power to take up the water in winter, that is, they are in the opposite state of "Su-Seung-Hwa-Kang," the leaves and fruits fall and the major life activity comes to a pause.

"Su-Seung-Hwa-Kang" is universal principle for the life activity in both nature and the human body. In the human body, the water energy is created in the kidneys and the fire energy is produced in the heart. When the water

Su-Seung-Hwa-Kang

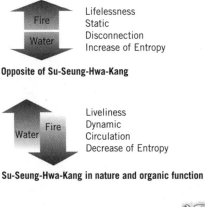

Fire
Water

Lifelessness
Static
Disconnection
Increase of Entropy

Opposite of Su-Seung-Hwa-Kang

Water   Fire

Liveliness
Dynamic
Circulation
Decrease of Entropy

Su-Seung-Hwa-Kang in nature and organic function

When the cosmic circulation activated, Dahn-Jon heats the kidney and pushes the water energy up. The water energy cools the heart and pushes its fire energy down to Dahn-Jon.

energy moves up through the Doc-Mak (Governor Meridian Channel) located in the middle of the back, the brain feels fresh and cool. The fire energy passing through the Im-Mak (Conception Meridian Channel) located in the middle of the chest down into the abdomen keeps the intestines warm.

A well functioning body in optimum health is like a house with the cooling system at the ceiling and the heating system near the floor. After restoring the body back into balance through the Dahnhak Practice, "Su-Seung-Hwa-Kang" is the natural state of a healthy body.

One sign that the body is in balance begins with tasting the saliva in the month. If it is sweet and fragrant, the body is in a state of "Su-Seung-Hwa-Kang." Another sign that the body is in balance is when the brain remains cool and fresh while the abdomen is warm and the intestines are working smoothly. The body is refreshed and energized.

A sign that the energy flow is reversed and the fire energy has become stagnant in the head is an occurrence of a headache. Then, the head feels hot and the body feels tired. The mouth feels dry and tastes bitter. The heart may feel heavy and beat irregularly. In this state, they feel tired, anxious and uncomfortable. Their shoulders and neck are stiff. This usually happens after a period of working or studying without moving around.

On the other hand, when there is no fire energy in the abdomen and the cold water energy is collecting in the intestines, most people suffer from digestive problems. The intestines are stiff. The abdomen is hard and painful to the touch. If the energy flow is not reversed soon, constipation results. It is like packing ice in the abdomen. Another sign that the water energy has moved to the abdomen instead of the fire energy is that a person experiences cold hands and feet. Men may also experience a lack of sexual stamina. If this condition continues, other medical complications may occur including high blood pressure or paralysis.

There are two major reasons that people experience the state opposite of "Su-Seung-Hwa-Kang." One is that they don't develop Dahn-Jon strongly enough to hold fire energy in the abdomen. In this state, when they use much energy in the brain, the fire energy goes up. The other reason is stress. When they suffer from stress and negative emotions, their Im-Mak is blocked, which reverses the normal flow of Ki and makes the fire energy go up. In this dysfunction, many neurotic diseases occur. When they recover the "Su-Seung-Hwa-Kang" state through the Dahn-hak Practice, all these chronic diseases are cured and optimum health is achieved.

"Su-Seung-Hwa-Kang" Exercises

"Su-Seung-Hwa-Kang" is achieved through Dahn-Jon Breathing which expels the used Ki-energy upon exhalation and accesses and accumulates new Ki-energy through inhalation. Dahn-Jon Breathing exercise is only effective if the intestines are soft and flexible. Most people, when they begin Dahnhak Practice, have stiff, hard abdomens. The Intestine Exercise remedies this condition by increasing the blood circulation to the intestines and by removing the problem of constipation.

Intestine Exercise

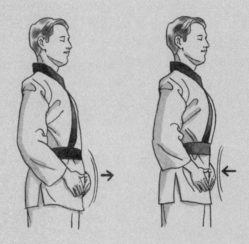

1) Place the hands on the abdomen, making a triangle with the thumbs and forefingers over the Ki-Hae.
2) Push the abdomen out.
3) Pull the abdomen in.
4) Repeat this movement 100 to 300 times in a rhythmic movement.
5) Begin gently and increase the repetitions slowly. If there is pain in the intestines during the exercise, stop and gently rub the abdomen in a circular motion, massaging the intestines with the palms.

Dahn-Jon Stimulation Exercise

Combined with the Intestine Exercise, the Dahn-Jon Stimulation Exercise will help the intestines become soft and flexible for Dahn-Jon Breathing. This exercise not only stimulates and softens the intestines but also awakens the Dahn-Jon.

1) Stand with the feet shoulder width apart.
2) Place the hands on the abdomen in the same position as the Intestine Exercise.
3) Instead of moving the abdomen in and out, begin patting the abdomen in a rhythmic motion with the palms.
4) Increase the pressure of the patting until it becomes a slapping motion. Continue this movement 100 to 300 times.
5) Begin gently and increase the repetitions slowly.

Jong-Chung, Ki-Jang, Shin-Myong: Health to Enlightenment

There are specific steps that people take when they move towards enlightenment.It is expressed by the phrase: "Jong-Chung, Ki-Jang, Shin-Myong."

Jong-Chung is the first step towards enlightenment. "Jong" means "vital energy" and "Chung" means "full." At first, a person becomes full of vital energy. This is accomplished through Dahn-Jon Breathing exercise.

Ki-Jang is the next step. "Ki" means "mental/emotional energy." "Jang" means "completion." When the mental energy reaches a stage of completion, the Middle Dahn-Jon is activated and the person experiences spontaneous love

Shin-Myong
Human Perfection
Fully awakened and enlightened consciousness
Disclosing all the mysteries about life and cosmos
Perfect peace and freedom
reintegration of the trinity
diminished need for sleep

Ki-Jang
Maturity of the Middle Dahn-Jon
Heart becoming wide-open
spontaneous love and joy, positivity and acceptance
Free from the compulsory desire for food

Jong-Chung
Completion of the Lower Dahn-Jon
Improvement of physical condition
Strengthened vitality
Power to control sexual drive

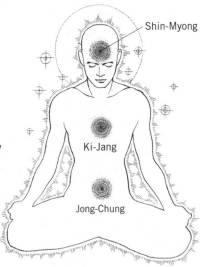

and joy.

Shin-Myong is the last step. "Shin" means "heavenly intelligence." "Myong" means "awakened." When the heavenly intelligence is awakened, the person has reached enlightenment and the goal of Dahnhak Practice, Human Perfection, has been reached.

Shim-Ki-Hyol-Jong: From Mind to Matter

The third principle deals with the process of materializing and dematerializing matter. The principle reflects the understanding of how material existence, including the universe, came into being and the direction all matter is ultimately going.

"Shim-Ki" means the mind (Shim) creates energy (Ki). All kinds of energy are the expression of the movements in the mind. The quality and power of the energy are determined by the mind. "Hyol" means "blood" and "Jong" means "matter." When the energy is condensed, it forms a vital force which is represented in the body by blood (Hyol).

Equilibrium before Mind moves

Mind moves and
creates an **Idea/Wish**

The Idea/Wish pulls **Energy**
to realize itself

Energy brings and organizes
the **Blood (Elements)**

The Idea/Wish **Materializes**

**The process of Evolution/Creation
which starts from a Idea/Wish and ends with a its Realization**

Blood or the vital force makes body or matter (Jong).

Wherever the mind goes, energy flows. When practitioners fully realize this and understand how to control the flow of energy according to the will, they are able to change mind into matter.

5. Dahn-Jon Breathing: Meditative Breathwork

The purpose of Dahn-Jon Breathing is to take vital cosmic Ki-energy into the body and accumulate it in the Dahn-Jon. The pure cosmic energy refreshes the mind and body.It also increases the natural healing power of the body by strengthening the immune system and supporting the functions of the organs in the body.

Dahn-Jon Breathing is a holistic meditative method of respiration.

Through Dahn-Jon Breathing, practitioners learn a technique that controls the energy flow in their bodies. Their minds are awakened into another dimension that has a wider and clearer perception. There is a higher understanding of the world and how they see themselves in the world. The universality of Ki in all of the seemingly different phenomena in the universe will become apparent. The world, the universe, will not be the same.

Dahn-Jon Breathing is a simple and effective method. It does not require a lot of training. Rather, it is the most natural way of breathing. A newborn baby knows how to practice Dahn-Jon Breathing. It is the way all babies breathe through the umbilical cord in their mother's wombs.

Dahn-Jon Breathing Exercise for Accumulating Ki-energy

The following meditation will assist practitioners in understanding the Dahn-Jon Breathing Exercise:

Imagine yourself as a child of the universe. Place yourself in the cosmic womb with your umbilical cord connected to the source of cosmic energy. With each inhalation, take in the cosmic energy through your umbilical cord. With each breath, feel how you are restored to the original Oneness with the mother cosmos.

The following is the important acupressure points in the Dahn-Jon Breathing exercise:

1) **Dahn-Jon**: Two inches below the navel and two inches inside the abdomen.
2) **Bak-Hoe**: Top of the head.
3) **Myong-Mun**: On the back, opposite the navel, between the 2nd and the 3rd lumbar vertebrae.
4) **Je-Jung**: At the navel, opposite the Myong-Mun.
5) **Ki-Hae**: About 2 inches below the navel.

The Location of the Lower Dahn-Jon

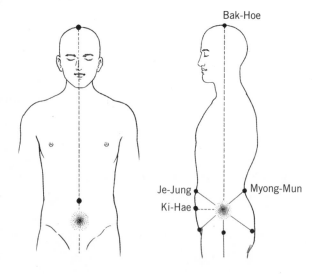

Bak-Hoe

Je-Jung
Ki-Hae

Myong-Mun

Dahn-Jon Breathing Exercise

1) **Preparing for Dahn-Jon Breathing**: Remove all tension from the body. If any tension remains in the body or mind at the beginning of the Dahn-Jon Breathing exercise, this may cause the fire energy to move from the chest into the head, resulting in a headache. Remove any trivial thoughts and concentrate fully on the Dahn-Jon Breathing.

2) **Feeling the warmth in the Dahn-Jon**: In Dahn-Jon Breathing, the Myong-Mun acts as the nose and the Dahn-Jon becomes the lungs. Inhale through Myong-Mun, gently expanding the abdomen. Then exhale, slowly pulling the abdomen inward. Again, inhale and push the abdomen gently out and down at a 45 degree angle. As you inhale, follow the flow of Ki-energy through the Myong-Mun and downward towards the Dahn-Jon. Visualize the Myong-Mun as the opening in the body and the abdomen as a balloon collecting the Ki. Begin to accumulate Ki-energy in the Dahn-Jon.

Do not force the breath. Breathing should be natural, directed by the movement of the abdomen. Keep the mind and body relaxed and comfortable. It is best to use only 80% the breathing capacity, when beginning this exercise.

For most people beginning the Dahn-Jon Breathing exercise, the Im-Mak (Conception Meridian Channel) is blocked and the intestines are stiff. Forcing the intake of air in the beginning may create breathing problems, pains in the chest or a headache. This is caused by blockages in the Im-Mak, forcing the fire energy in the chest into the head instead of the abdomen. To improve the effectiveness of Dahn-Jon Breathing exercise, breathe moderately and practice the intestine exercise daily.

At first, there may not be any sensation in the Dahn-Jon. This may be due to the energy channel being blocked or the sense of Ki not being fully developed. With practice, the warmth of the energy moving inside the abdomen will become apparent. When there is a feeling of the heat in the abdomen, the Dahn-Jon has been identified. Concentrate on that point. As the awareness of the Dahn-Jon increases, more energy and heat will be felt. The sense of heat may change into a magnetic or electric sensation.

When the Dahn-Jon feels warm, imagine an energy ball in the Dahn-Jon. Deepen the breathing and the energy ball will become larger. Soon the abdominal area will be filled with the ball of energy.

3) **Visualizing the movement of Ki-energy**: As the warmth in the Dahn-Jon increases, inhale visualizing the Ki-energy flowing in through the Myong-Mun towards the Dahn-Jon, accumulating in a spiraling motion within the Dahn-Jon like the shell of a snail. Then, exhale, following the flow of Ki in a straight line from the Dahn-Jon to the

Myong-Mun and out the back. There will be a stream of energy flowing along the channel between the two points. During this exercise, the large and small intestines might automatically start moving as they soften and purify.

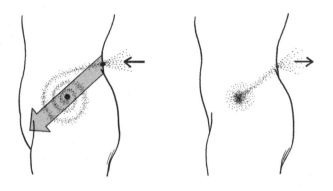

Two Positions for Dahn-Jon Breathing Exercise

1) Lying Down

Most beginners start Dahn-Jon Breathing exercise lying down. This position is also recommended for anyone who feels ill or weak. Lying down makes Dahn-Jon Breathing easier especially when exhausted or just before or after sleeping.

To begin, lie down on the back in a comfortable position with the feet shoulder width apart. Place both hands on the Lower Dahn-Jon with thumbs and index fingers forming a triangle around the Ki-Hae. Close your eyes. Gently close the mouth. Relax all the muscles in the face. Relax the entire body.

2) Sitting Up

Sit in a lotus or half lotus position. Straighten the spine with hips tilted backward slightly. Relax the shoulders and arms. Place the hands on the knees with the palms up. (It is advisable to bring the tip of the thumb, index and middle fingers together.) Or, put both hands on the Dahn-Jon to form a triangle around the Ki-Hae. Relax the muscles of the chest.

6. Signs of Healing: Jin-Dong and Myong-Hyon

Jin-Dong: Vibration of Life in the Meridian Channel

For practitioners, fundamental changes occur in the body during the exercises. The changes differ from one person to the next. Without some understanding of what is happening to the body as a result of the Ki-energy stimulation, some people might feel frightened or even at a loss when they experience Jin-Dong.

One of the signs that the body is changing is when the body begins to shake. This reaction is the result of a person moving into a deeply relaxed, alpha brain wave state. Jin-Dong can best be described as suddenly opening a water faucet connected to a garden hose. With the increase in water pressure, the hose begins to shake violently. This is similar to the first opening of energy paths previously blocked by stagnant energy.

As a person begins to feel the flow of energy circulating throughout the body, the body will often shake vigorusly (like the garden hose) as blockades in the meridian channels are cleared by the new flood of energy.

There are two types of Jin-Dong. In one case, Jin-Dong occurs when a sufficient accumulation of energy is reached and begins to flow rapidly through the meridian system. In another case, Jin-Dong can result from an influx of vital cosmic energy, after a person has fully opened the mind.

Practitioners with good energy circulation may not experience Jin-Dong at first. But eventually, every practitioner experiences Jin-Dong, the vibration of life. In some cases, practitioners may not know that they are experiencing Jin-Dong because the vibration is so delicate. When individuals persist with the practice and certain parts of the body are revitalized, even healthy people can experience Jin-Dong.

Jin-Dong can be experienced as a continuous vibration for a certain period of time. Then, it will begin to weaken gradually and eventually completely stop. When practitioners experience Jin-Dong, there is a temptation to become preoccupied with this phenomena. However, spending too much time absorbed in this phenomena will exhaust anyone.

Jin-Dong can be controlled consciously since it is related to being in a state of relaxation from the lowering of brain waves. Jin-Dong is a sign that Dahnhak Practice is reaching a plateau. After an experience of Jin-Dong, most people feel refreshed and amiable since the blocked meridian channels have been opened. The mind feels steady and strong. A person's health improves after such an experience.

Myong-Hyon: Alternating Brightness and Darkness

Myong-Hyon is another healing phenomena as common as Jin-Dong. The first sign of Myong-Hyon begins when practitioners develop cold-like symptoms or their bodies feel tired, weak or heavy.

For practitioners with health problems, the symptoms may be more severe. Sometimes, practitioners may experience a recurrence of a health problem. When this happens, it is a sign that the chronic health problem is being cured. As in Jin-Dong, the cause of this phenomena is blockages in the flow of Ki-energy.

The symptoms will persist until the energy flow is clear. When this happens, the Ki-energy will wash out the toxins from the body which the stagnant energy held.

The word "Myong" means brightness, and "Hyon" means darkness. Thus, Myong-Hyon means "alternating brightness and darkness." Experiencing cyclical changes in the body's condition, alternating between feeling good and feeling bad, means the body is returning to good health. When practitioners experience poor physical responses, this indicates that the body is moving towards better health.

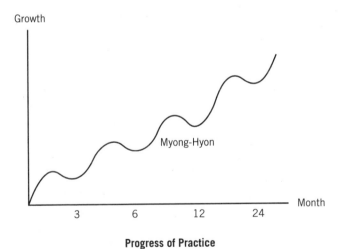

Progress of Practice

Chon-Ji-Ki-Un
(Highest Level of Energy)

Chon-Ji-Ki-Un brings health to the body and peace to the mind.

Chon-Ji-Ki-Un heals grief and loneliness.

Chon-Ji-Ki-Un fills the mind with confident quietude and fertilizes the heart with love and joy.

Chon-Ji-Ki-Un gives the power to forgive even the unforgivable.

Chon-Ji-Ki-Un produces no fright and no fear.

Chon-Ji-Ki-Un knows nothing of victim-consciousness, selfishness, or arrogance.

Chon-Ji-Ki-Un encourages honesty, trustworthiness and responsibility.

Chon-Ji-Ki-Un is the pure cosmic energy guiding seekers to eternal life through enlightening the spirit and raising the soul.

Chon-Ji-Ma-Um
(Enlightened Consciousness)

Chon-Ji-Ma-Um is the originator of Chon-Ji-Ki-Un.
Chon-Ji-Ki-Un is the carrier of Chon-Ji-Ma-Um.
Chon-Ji-Ki-Un is the Body of Chon-Ji-Ma-Um.
Chon-Ji-Ma-Um is the Mind of Chon-Ji-Ki-Un.
Chon-Ji-Ma-Um creates ideas.
Chon-Ji-Ki-Un realizes ideas.
Chon-Ji-Ma-Um motivates Chon-Ji-Ki-Un.
Chon-Ji-Ki-Un empowers Chon-Ji-Ma-Um.
Chon-Ji-Ki-Un resides in Chon-Ji-Ma-Um
Chon-Ji-Ma-Um lives on Chon-Ji-Ki-Un.
Each is the gate to the other.
Their duality makes their oneness alive and creative.

* Two poems sum up the relationship of Chon-Ji-Ki-Un (Highest Level of Energy) and Chon-Ji-Ma-Um (Enlightened Consciousness) experienced by practitioners.

DAHNHAK PRACTICE

1. The Steps of Dahnhak Practice

Dahnhak consists of five steps that teach the participant to use the breath to control the mind and bring Ki-energy into the body:

1) Initiating
2) Accumulating
3) Controlling
4) Commanding
5) Completing

Most practitioners quickly experience the benefits of optimum health including the healing of chronic illnesses. With the understanding of the relationship between body and Ki-energy, along with beginning to control their body, practitioners feel happier about themselves. As the Dahnhak Practice continues, they begin to comprehend experientially the basic principles of the universe and life, and finally reach the goal of Dahnhak: ultimate freedom and Human Perfection.

The following is a brief outline of the five steps and their benefits to the practitioners:

1) Initiating: The Dahnhak Practice begins with experiencing Ki-energy. The "Do-In" and "Ji-Gam" exercises help the beginners feel Ki-energy, relax their bodies and discover their inner consciousness. The results are improved physical condition, enhanced concentration, and freedom from anxiety and stress.

2) Accumulating: At this step, the Lower Dahn-Jon is

developed and Ki-energy is accumulated in the Lower Dahn-Jon.

The following exercises are taught: "Dahn-Jon Breathing." "Hang-Gong," "Un-Ki-Shim-Gong," "Dahn-Mu," and "Dahn-Gong." Practitioners benefit from these exercises which support the healthy functioning of the internal organs and the removal of toxins from the body. The natural healing power of the body is activated, thus, removing many physical problems that might have existed prior to the start of the Dahnhak Practice. As a result of feeling better, people also begin to feel more self-confident and start practicing positive thinking.

3) **Controlling**: During this step, the Middle Dahn-Jon is awakened. The result is an experience of habitual joy and peace. The Hang-Gong exercise in which the Ki-energy is circulated through the Dae-Mak (Girdle Meridian Channel), Im-Mak (Conception Meridian Channel), and Doc-Mak (Governor Meridian Channel) is introduced. An immediate result is the spontaneous correction of any misalignment of the body structure. Interpersonal relationships begin to change as a result of the practitioner's new image of themselves. And in some cases, people stop addictive behaviors such as smoking, drinking and drugs.

4) **Commanding**: At this point, all the meridian channels in the body are opened. The connection to the Microcosmic Energy Circuit of the universe is completed. The Upper Dahn-Jon is awakened. Practitioners understand the mysteries of life, experience unconditional love and feel an increase in creativity. The practitioners can access their potential and achieve their goals. The body and mind are totally purified and integrated. And each practitioner can use his/her physical, mental and spiritual powers to benefit one's neighbors and the whole humankind.

5) Completing: At this step the practitioners achieve the goal of Dahnhak which is Human Perfection. The illusion of ego is released and replaced by identification with True Self. There is a realization of the Oneness of all existence. The ability to live in harmony and unity with the cosmic trinity-Heaven, Earth and Human-becomes a reality. As the Macrocosmic Energy Circuit stabilizes, practitioners feel the true Nothingness, which is the unification of the cosmic trinity. Their minds become one with the Cosmos. They experience free Ki-energy communication with Nature.

2. Practitioner's Memorandum

The following attitudes are most helpful when practicing Dahnhak:

1) **Focus**: Remember the purpose of Dahnhak Practice and maintain a positive outlook.

2) **Relax**: Remove all tension, which inhibits concentration, from the body and mind.

3) **Concentrate**: Harmonize the breath with the mind.

4) **Observe**: Observe the response of the body and changes to the body.

5) **Communicate**: Sincerely and honestly converse with the body to encourage the body to listen to the mind.

6) **Practice**: Make Dahnhak Practice part of a daily routine, including Dahn-Jon Breathing before going to bed, after waking up and during breaks in the day's activities.

7) **Appreciate**: Develop a thankful and delightful mind to encourage harmony between the body and mind.

3. Recommendations

For effective and efficient results from the Dahnhak Practice, here are some suggestions:

1) **Practice Daily**: Regular practice brings about rapid changes in the body and mind. Make time for the practice and do it regularly.

2) **Cultivate Moderate Emotional Responses**: The human body and mind are affected by the emotions. Different emotional responses affect different parts of the body. The stomach is weakened by stress, lungs by sadness, kidneys by fear, heart by excessive excitement, liver by anger. Excessive anger will deplete energy reserves and exhaust the body.

3) **Refrain from Excessive Drinking, Excessive Sex, Overeating and Overwork**: The Ki-energy accumulated in the body will be dissipated by overindulgence. Excessive drinking and eating exhaust the digestive organs and reduce the recovery time between meals. Excessive sex and workaholism stress the organs in the body by dissipating the energy gained from the Dahnhak Practice.

4) **Master the Basic Practice**: Practicing the basic exercises, which are important building blocks for further work in Dahnhak, will produce strong, deep and powerful results.

5) **Live a Harmonious Life**: The purpose of Dahnhak Practice is to discover and enjoy a meaningful life secured on a strong foundation of a healthy mind and body. Practitioners are cooperative, kind and devoted to their family and friends.

4. Basic Dahnhak Exercises

Do-In Exercise: Meridian Exercise

"Do" means "lead or pull the Ki-energy into the body." "In" means "stretching." Do-In Exercise is a systematic stretching exercise that helps the mind and body relax before beginning Dahn-Jon Breathing and other exercises.

Most people have the habit of using only certain parts of their body, not moving their whole body. Limited body movements create stiffness and blockages to the Ki-energy flow. This becomes evident when practitioners are asked to feel the Ki-energy moving through their bodies during Dahn-Jon Breathing exercise. The Do-In Exercise helps relieve stiffness and gets the Ki-energy flowing.

Compared to other stretching exercises, Do-In Exercise combines proper breathing with stretching movements. When breath is combined with body movement, the circulation of Ki-energy can be felt more easily. Breathing helps the body purify toxins which have accumulated due to lack of exercise or deep relaxed breathing. Breathing deeply into the lower abdomen makes the stretching exercises easier and the sensation of Ki-energy more apparent.

While practicing the stretching movements of Do-In Exercise, practitioners should concentrate on the Lower Dahn-Jon. As concentration levels increase, the Dahn-Jon feels warmer, and deeper states of consciousness are accessed.

The Do-In Exercise encourages people to move all

their muscles and stretch their spines. This stimulates the brain, realigns the spine and helps the body reestablish a natural symmetrical balance.

A feeling of positive energy and the release of tension in the body are two of the results of the Do-In Exercise. The internal organs are stimulated. The muscles, nerves and circulation system are strengthened. Finally, the meridian system is activated, revitalizing the entire body. All feelings of stress and fatigue disappear.

To experience the best results from the Do-In Exercise, the following breathing sequence should be followed: take a deep breath at the beginning of each movement, hold the breath throughout the stretch and breathe out slowly as the exercise is completed. If a person suffers from high blood pressure or poor health due to age, the following breathing sequence should be followed. Instead of holding the breath during the stretch, the breath should be exhaled. The practice of Do-In Exercise assists the body in accumulating Ki-energy in the Dahn-Jon, benefitting the entire body.

Do-In Exercise should become part of the practitioner's daily program. There are three positions for the Do-In Exercise: lying down, sitting or standing. Listed below are the basic forms of Do-In Exercise:

Chon-Hyong (Heaven Form)

This section of the Do-In Exercise is called Heaven Form, reminding practitioners to follow the shape of the sky above. Use rounded half circle motions during the movements imitating the half dome shape of the sky. The following are 14 basic forms of Chon-Hyong Do-In Exercise.

1) Body Bounce

Stand with the legs shoulder width apart. Bend the knees slightly and begin to bounce gently. Move the arms from the armpits down along the side of the body. Rhythmically bounce the entire body up and down. This movement activates the smooth functioning of the intestines.

2) Arm Twist

With arms stretched out to the side of the body at shoulder height, begin twisting the arms forward and backward. Twist the left hand forward, turning the entire arm, while at the same time, twist the right hand backward, turning the entire right arm in the same direction. Repeat the movement, with the right hand forward and the left hand backward. This movement eliminates tension in the shoulders and any numbness in the arms.

3) Neck Stretch

With your hands on your waist, drop your head forward and down towards your chest, as far as you can. Feel the stretch through the back of your neck, and then drop your head backward. Repeat this couple of times. Move the head to the left side and try to touch the left ear to the shoulder. Repeat the movement in the opposite direction, trying to touch the right ear to the right shoulder. Bring your head upright and rest. Next, rotate your head to the left side. Repeat the movement in the opposite direction. Headaches can be moderated or stopped as a result of this movement.

4) Knee Bounce and Rotation

Place the knees together and bend them slightly. With the hands on the top of the knees, begin gently bouncing. Next, rotate the knees, together, in a circular

1)

2)

3)

4)

5)

motion towards the right. Repeat the movement in the opposite direction. This movement will strengthen the knee joints and help prevent arthritis.

5) Leg and Upper Body Stretch

With feet together, bend over at the waist and touch the hands to the floor. Repeat the motion, with the hands crossed and touch the floor with a gentle bouncing motion. This movement increases flexibility for the back of the legs, thighs, back, spine and arms, stimulating the Doc-Mak.

6) Hip Joint Rotation

Standing with the legs shoulder width apart, raise the left leg with the knee bent. Slowly rotate the knee in a clockwise motion giving the hip joint a good stretch. Repeat the motion in a counterclockwise motion. Repeat the movement with the right leg in both directions. This movement gives a good stretch to the hip joints and helps maintain balance.

7) Side Stretch

Sitting on the floor, open the legs as wide as possible. Place the left hand on the right side of the waist. Move the right hand over the top of the head stretching to the left and touch the left toe. Repeat this movement for the opposite side of the body. This movement stimulates the bladder and kidneys.

8) Sam-Um-Gyo Stimulation

Sitting on the floor with legs bent and feet together, press with the thumbs the Sam-Um-Gyo, the acupressure point located on the inside of the leg, just above the ankle. This movement stimulates and strengthens the kidneys, spleen, and liver. This exercise is especially beneficial for women.

9) Upper Body Bend

Sitting on the floor, place the soles of the feet together. Bend at the waist with a gentle bouncing movement until the forehead touches the floor. Then, turn the head to the left touching the right ear to the floor. Then turn the head to the right touching the left ear to the floor. This movement increases flexibility the hip joints and waist.

10) Jok-Sam-Ri Pat

Sitting on the floor with legs bent, gently pat the Jok-Sam-Ri, the acupressure point located on the outside of the leg, just below the knee, and in-between where the two leg bones meet. This movement strengthens the stomach and stops headaches.

11) Spine Roll

Sitting on the floor, bend the knees up to the chest and clasp the arms around the legs. Round the back so that the forehead is against the knees. Gently roll back until the back is on the floor and then, forward to the starting position, sitting up. This movement helps the spine become more flexible and stimulates the organs throughout the body.

12) Leg Shake

Lie on the floor and raise both legs with the soles of the feet facing the ceiling. Shake the legs vigorously. This movement increases blood circulation and loosens tight leg muscles.

13) Waist Rotation

Sit in a half lotus position on the floor with the spine straight. Rotate the waist to the left and then to the right for the flexibility throughout the waist. This movement stimulates the intestines.

14) Dahn-Jon Pat

Sitting with the legs crossed, pat the Lower Dahn-Jon. Increase the strength of the patting, until the fists are

12)

13)

14)

pounding the Lower Dahn-Jon vigorously to vibrate the intestines deep inside the abdominal area. This movement stimulates the blood circulation to the intestines and the Lower Dahn-Jon.

Ji-Hyong (Earth Form)

This section of the Do-In Exercise refers to the strength and support of the earth. It is called Earth Form to remind the practitioner to develop strength in the body like the power of the earth. The following are 14 basic forms of Ji-Hyong Do-In Exercise.

1) Arm Throw
With legs shoulder width apart, throw the arms to the sides like splashing the water from your fingers. Repeat the same motion forward, upward, and downward. This exercise reduces any pain in the neck or shoulders and warms cold fingertips.

2) Arm Clasp and Twist

Standing with legs shoulder width apart, stretch the arms out in front of the body. Twist the arms and clasp the palms together so that the wrists are crossed. Bring the clasped hands towards the chest, then straighten the arms out in front of the body. Continuing to clasp hands, bend backwards for a good stretch. This stretch relaxes the shoulders, elbows, wrists, and shoulder blades while stimulating the thyroid gland.

3) Half Knee Stretch

Bend the right knee and turn the right foot to the left at a 45 degree angle. Straighten the left knee with the heel on the floor and the toes pointing upward. Put hands on the knees, and bounce gently towards the left knee. Repeat the same movement for the opposite side. This movement provides a good stretch for the knee joints.

4) Full Knee Stretch

Open your legs wide. Bend the right knee and stretch the left leg out straight to the left of the body, with heel on the floor and toes pointing upward. Place the hands on the knees. Gently bounce towards the left knee. Repeat this motion for the opposite leg. This movement helps relax the hip joints and any tightness in the leg muscles.

5) Thigh Stretch

Bend the right knee and stretch the left leg out behind the body. Place the left hand on the floor and the right hand on the right knee. Gently bounce to gain flexibility. Repeat this motion for the opposite leg. This movement will stretch the thighs, reduce tension in the legs and prevent bowing of the legs.

6) Lower Back Stretch

Stand with legs a little more than shoulder width apart and hands clasped with palms together. Raise the left knee and move it to the right while, at the same time, twisting the clasped arms to the left. Repeat this motion in the opposite direction. This movement twists and stretches the lumbar vertebrae and also, tones the waist muscles.

7) Waist Rotation

Standing with legs shoulder width apart, place both hands on the waist. Rotate the hips to the right. Repeat this motion in the opposite direction. This movement increases flexibility for the waist muscles and hip joints, assisting the body in keeping balance.

8) Arm Stretch

Stand with the legs shoulder width apart and clasp hands with the palms facing outward. With hands clasped, straighten the arms over the head and pull the arms backwards. Repeat this motion forward, to the left, and to the right. This movement relaxes the shoulder blades and arm muscles.

6)

7)

8)

9) Side Stretch

Stand with both legs shoulder width apart and clasp hands together with the palms facing outward. Raise arms over the head and bend, first, to the left as far as possible, and then, to the right. This movement stretches the side of the body.

10) Standing Upper Body Bend

Stand with legs shoulder width apart and clasp hands behind the back. Straighten the arms and stretch. Bend forward at the waist in a bouncing motion with the head forward. Bring the arms up behind the back and stretch. This movement makes the spine flexible and corrects any problems with vertebrae.

11) Waist Twist

Sitting on the floor, Place the hands on the floor and bend the knees together to the left. Twist the upper body and head to the right, looking in the opposite direction from the knees. Repeat the motion in the opposite direction. This movement increases flexibility for the waist.

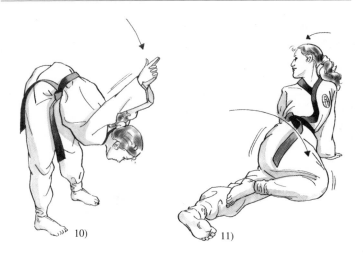

12) Waist Stretch

Sitting on the floor with legs outstretched in a comfortable open position. Twist the waist and upper body to the left side until the head is facing towards the back. Place the hands on the floor. Bend the upper body so that the right ear can touch the floor. Repeat the motion in the opposite direction. This movement gives the waist a good stretch and releases tension in the legs.

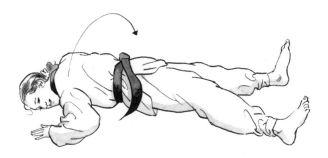

13) Sitting Upper Body Bend #1

Sitting on the floor, with legs forward and together,

bend at the waist and touch the toes. If touching the toes is difficult, touch the knees. Gently bounce forward and touch the chest to the thighs. This movement strengthens the bladder and reduces fatigue.

14) Sitting Upper Body Bend #2

Sitting on the floor, with the legs forward and open wide, bend at the waist and touch the floor between the legs. Gently bounce forward and touch the chest to the floor.

In-Hyong (Human Form)

This section of the Do-In Exercise is called the Human Form reminding practitioners to develop a harmonious relationship with their partners.

1) Face to Face Hand Clap
Face each other with hands raised and palms facing. Clap the hands together, letting the arms fall downwards. Smile. This movement stimulates all of the internal organs and increases blood circulation in the shoulders and arms.

2) Back to Back Hand Clap
Standing back to back about one foot apart, clap hands in front of the body. Move the hands outside and back, clap hands with the partner. Repeat this motion. This movement relaxes the shoulders and shoulder blades.

3) Back to Back Waist Twist

Stand back to back about three feet apart. Bend the knees. Twist to one side and clap the hands together. Repeat the motion in the opposite direction. This movement relaxes the waist and upper body.

4) Back to Back Squat

Stand back to back with arms interlaced at the elbows. Together sit down and stand up, using the force of pressing against each other. This movement strengthens the lower body. The success of this exercise is dependent upon each partner remaining in balance. Only when both partners are in harmony and communication, is the exercise possible.

5) Face to Face Squat

Facing each other and standing about two feet apart, clasp each other's wrists. In unison, sit down and stand up using the force of leaning back a little from each other. This movement cultivates endurance and strengthens the leg muscles.

3)

4)

5)

6) Face to Face Hand Push

Standing three feet apart with palms touching, push one hand and pull the other while remaining upright. This movement cultivates endurance and strengthens the lower body.

7) Side to Side Wrist Lock

Stand three feet apart side by side facing away from the partner. Clasping each other's wrist, alternately push and pull each other while remaining upright and balanced. Repeat the movement after switching sides. This move-

6)

7)

ment strengthens the muscles in the arms.

8) Face to Face Bridge

Face each other with legs spread apart. Place hands on the partner's shoulders. Bend forward at the waist. Bounce together. This movement relaxes the shoulders and waist.

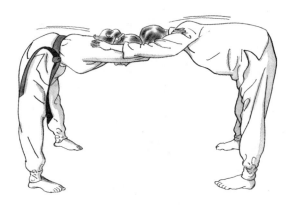

9) Side to Side Arm Arch

Standing side by side with legs spread apart, face the same direction with the outside leg bent and the inside leg straight. Clasp hands with the outside hands arched over the head. Gently pull the waist, arms, and legs. This movement relaxes the shoulders and waist.

10) Back to Back Twirl

Stand back to back, with backs touching. Stretch the arms out to the side and clasp hands. Begin a twirling motion in one direction, moving together like a revolving fan. Repeat the motion in the opposite direction. This movement relaxes the muscles of the waist, arms, and back.

Ji-Gam Exercise: Ki-energy Awareness Exercise

Ji-Gam exercise introduces the awareness of Ki-energy through direct experience. It is a meditative exercise which develops the sixth sense so that practitioners can feel the invisible Ki-energy. The first step towards feeling Ki-energy is to acknowledge that Ki-energy exists. This invisible bio-energy is not tangible. It cannot be observed through the five senses: smell, sound, sight, touch, and taste. A sensitivity, which most people call the sixth sense, is necessary to understand the existence of this energy.

"Ji-Gam" means detaching from outer consciousness of the five senses and going into the inner consciousness of the sixth sense. With concentration and a willingness to discover another level of awareness, Ki-energy is accessible through Ji-Gam.

Ji-Gam Exercise focuses on the hands because the hands are the most sensitive part of the body. Jin-Ki, the essence of all energy, is most easily activated through the hands.

1) Sitting in a half lotus posture with both hands resting on the top of the knees, close the eyes and relax, releasing any tension in the body. Check the neck and shoulders to see if all the tension has been released.
2) Lift both hands slowly from the knees, and place the palms together chest high.
3) With the eyes closed, try to see the hands with the mind's eye. Concentrate on the feeling in the hands, noticing any subtle sensations.
4) After a while, the hands may begin to feel warm. Feel

the blood moving through the hands from the heart. Listen to the heartbeat in the hands. Feel the pulsation of the blood moving through the hands. Silently, call out to the hands: hands! hands! hands! Notice if there is any other sensation in the hands.

5) Slowly separate the palms until they are about two inches apart. Let go of all tension. Make sure the shoulders are relaxed. Relax the hands so that they feel suspended in the air in front of the chest. Begin to notice the strong energy field between the hands. With the mind's eye, look at the hands, and imagine the Ki-energy between the palms. It may look like light or a cloud. Is it bright and full, floating like a slowly moving cloud?

6) Widen the distance between the palms. Concentrate on the change of Ki-energy as the hands move farther apart. The sensation may be warm, electric, or magnetic. For each person, the sensation is a little different: very subtle or quite strong like soft Jell-O; like being under water or in a gentle breeze.

7) The hands may feel like magnets, pulling or pushing the palms. This sensation may be subtle at first and then, grow stronger and clearer with concentration.

8) When the feeling of the Ki-energy becomes strong, move the palms farther apart. Follow the flow of Ki-energy with the hands, enjoying the feeling of this life-giving energy.

Hang-Gong Exercise: Dahn-Jon Breathing Postures

Hang-Gong is an essential part of Dahnhak Practice. This series of exercises is composed of static postures designed to facilitate deep Dahn-Jon Breathing. Moving past the traditional half and full lotus postures for meditation, practitioners deepen their meditation practice by adopting radically different, non-traditional postures. These expanded meditation poses fortify the meridian system and improve the body's self-healing mechanisms.

Hang-Gong consists of 9 levels, with 5 different postures for each level. The flow of Ki-energy develops in the body in a way similar to the growth of the human body. Hang-Gong imitates the process of a baby lying on its back, sucking toes,turning over, crawling, sitting, and standing up alone. With each successive posture, the flow of Ki-energy increases in the body. The more Hang-Gong poses achieved, the faster and deeper the Ki-energy flows through the body.

Hang-Gong starts at level 9 and moves towards level 1. The deep Dahn-Jon Breathing combined with the Hang-Gong poses produces the surprising results of joy and well-being.

Hang-Gong Level 9

The 9th level of Hang-Gong focuses on the deep relaxation of the body. In a totally relaxed state, practitioners develop deep abdominal breathing and experience the flow of Ki through the body. Hang-Gong Level 9 helps the autonomic nervous system relax, releasing tension and anxiety. It also relaxes any tight muscles around the spinal column.

1) Posture 1

Lie down in a comfortable position with the legs shoulder width apart. Place the hands on the Lower Dahn-Jon, creating a triangle by touching thumb to thumb and

index finger to index finger.

Practice: As the breathing slows down, consciously relax the body beginning at the top of the head moving to the tip of the toes. With the mind's eye, visualize the basic path of the Ki-energy flow: face, neck, chest, abdomen, Lower Dahn-Jon, shoulders, elbows, hands, Lower Dahn-Jon, thighs, knees, calves, ankles and toes.

2) Posture 2

Slowly bend the left leg up and place the left foot beside the right knee. Make a fist with the right hand, thumb inside, and place it underneath the back of the neck. Place the left hand on the Lower Dahn-Jon.

Practice: Concentrate on the Ki-energy flow in the body: face, neck, chest, abdomen, Lower Dahn-Jon, left shoulder, left elbow, left hand, Lower Dahn-Jon, right thigh, right knee, right calf, right ankle, right foot, right toes. Placing the fist under the base of the skull prevents the fire energy and its warmth from moving into the head.

3) Posture 3

Reverse the leg and hand positions of Posture 2.

Practice: Concentrate on the Ki-energy flow in the body: face, neck, chest, abdomen, Lower Dahn-Jon, right shoulder, right elbow, right hand, Lower Dahn-Jon, left thigh, left knee, left calf, left ankle, left foot, left toes.

4) Posture 4

Bend both knees with the feet shoulder width apart. Place the left hand on the Lower Dahn-Jon and the right fist at the back of the neck as in Posture 2.

Practice: Concentrate on the Ki-energy flow in the

body: face, neck, chest, abdomen, Lower Dahn-Jon, left shoulder, left elbow, left hand, Lower Dahn-Jon, both thighs, both knees, both calves, both ankles, both feet, both toes, both soles, both calves, both knees, both thighs, back to the Lower Dahn-Jon.

5) Posture 5

Remaining in the same position with both knees bent and feet on the floor, reverse the hand position to right hand on the Lower Dahn-Jon and left fist at the back of the neck as in Posture 3.

Practice: Concentrate on the Ki-energy flow in the body: face, neck, chest, abdomen, Lower Dahn-Jon, right shoulder, right elbow, right hand, Lower Dahn-Jon, both thighs, both knees, both calves, both ankles, both feet, both toes, both soles, both calves, both knees, both thighs, back to the Lower Dahn-Jon.

Hang-Gong Level 8

The purpose of Hang-Gong Level 8 is to accumulate the maximum amount of Ki-energy in the body and strengthen the lower part of the body. During this practice, Ki-energy is accessed through the Jang-Shim and Yong-Chon and stored in the Lower Dahn-Jon.

1) Posture 1

Lie comfortably on the back, with the left leg raised and the knee bent at a 90 degree angle. Bend the ankle 90 degrees. Place both hands on the Lower Dahn-Jon, creating a triangle with the thumbs and index fingers.

Practice: Concentrate on the Ki-energy flow in the body: face, neck, chest, abdomen, Lower Dahn-Jon, shoulders, elbows, hands, Lower Dahn-Jon, right thigh, right knee, right calf, right ankle, right foot, right toes, left Yong-Chon, left ankle, left calf, left knee, left thigh, Lower Dahn-Jon.

Begin Dahn-Jon Breathing. While inhaling, allow the Ki-energy to flow from the left Yong-Chon to Dahn-Jon, and while exhaling, release the stale, used energy from the Dahn-Jon out through the right toes.

2) Posture 2

With the right leg, repeat the same position as described in Posture 1.

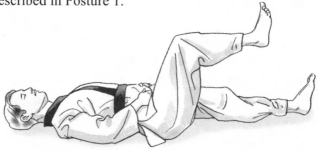

Practice: For the opposite side of the body, repeat practice described in Posture 1.

3) Posture 3

With both legs raised and knees bent at a 90 degree angle, bend ankles 90 degrees. Place both hands on the Lower Dahn-Jon, creating a triangle with the thumbs and index fingers.

Practice: Concentrate on the Ki-energy flow in the body: face, neck, chest, abdomen, Lower Dahn-Jon, shoulders, elbows, hands, Lower Dahn-Jon, thighs, knees, calves, ankles, feet, toes, Yong-Chon, ankles, calves, knees, thighs, Lower Dahn-Jon.

Do Dahn-Jon Breathing. Upon inhaling, let cosmic vitality flow into two Yong-Chons and up to the Lower Dahn-Jon. Upon exhaling, discharge the used energy from the Dahn-Jon out through the toes of the feet.

4) Posture 4

Continue to hold the legs in the same position as in Posture 3. Lift the arms straight up, perpendicular to the floor, with the palms facing the ceiling.

Practice: Concentrate on the energy flow in the body: face, neck, shoulders, elbows, hands, chest, abdomen,

Lower Dahn-Jon, thighs, knees, calves, ankles, feet, toes, Yong-Chons, ankles, calves, knees, thighs, Lower Dahn-Jon.

Do Dahn-Jon Breathing. Upon inhaling, let the cosmic energy enter through both Jang-Shims and Yong-Chons into the Lower Dahn-Jon. Upon exhaling, let the used Ki-energy flow out of the body through the same energy points.

5) Posture 5

Slowly lower the legs to the floor. Cross the ankles with the knees bent and the feet under the legs. Place the hands on the Dahn-Jon, making a triangle with thumbs and index fingers.

Practice: Continue the Dahn-Jon Breathing and become aware of any sensations in the Lower Dahn-Jon and Myong-Mun.

Hang-Gong Level 7

The purpose of level 7 is to accumulate Ki-energy in the Lower Dahn-Jon to achieve better physical health. The level 7 postures will also encourage muscle tone to strengthen the legs and waist. The Yong-Chon is greatly stimulated, which activates the rejuvenation of the kidneys and bladder.

Upon successful achievement of the postures, practitioners can access a deeper meditative state. In this state, the Ki-energy can be consciously moved to certain parts of the body or circulated throughout the body.

1) Posture 1

Lie comfortably on the back and place both hands on the Lower Dahn-Jon. With the right leg remaining on the floor, slowly pull the left leg up towards the chest with the left knee bent. Exhale and straighten the leg at an angle between 45 and 15 degrees from the floor depending upon the muscle strength in the abdomen.

Practice: Begin the Dahn-Jon Breathing cycle. When inhaling, Ki-energy flows into the Dahn-Jon through Myong-Mun. When exhaling, the stale Ki-energy moves down the left leg and out through the left Yong-Chon.

2) Posture 2

With the right leg, repeat the same position as described in Posture 1.

Practice: For the opposite side of the body, repeat practice described in Posture 1.

3) Posture 3

Inhale and slowly pull both legs up towards the chest with both knees bent, then straighten both legs at a 45 degree angle. Exhale and straighten both legs at an angle between 45 and 15 degrees from the floor.

Practice: Begin the Dahn-Jon Breathing and while exhaling, breathe the stale Ki-energy down both legs and out both Yong-Chons.

4) Posture 4

While repeating Posture 3, stretch both arms straight up, perpendicular to the floor, with the palms facing the ceiling.

Practice: Continue the Dahn-Jon Breathing as in Posture 3.

5) Posture 5

Repeat Hang-Gong Level 8, Posture 5.

Practice: Continue the Dahn-Jon Breathing as in Hang-Gong Level 8, Posture 5.

Un-Ki-Shim-Gong: Conscious Control of Ki-energy

"Un" means "circulation," "Ki" means "energy,", "Shim" means "consciousness" and "Gong" means "art." In other words, "Un-Ki-Shim-Gong" is "the art of circulating Ki-energy with the power of the mind or consciousness." This is an important and essential method to control and utilize Ki-energy throughout the body.

The exercise focuses on extremely slow and relaxed movements of the arms and hands called "the motionless-motion." The movements are like clouds floating through the sky or the slow, persistent blooming of a flower. This exercise will enable practitioners to relax and focus on the peace, joy and positive attitudes arising from the exercise

As practitioners advance through various levels, the experience of Ki-energy expands. Some experiences of Ki-energy defy description. During Un-Ki-Shim-Gong, the major acupressure points in the body become activated. Within this process, practitioners may begin to experience the body melting or even disappearing into the void of the universe. When all the acupressure points in the body become unobstructed and are wide open, Ki-energy flows freely in and out of the body. Practitioners will feel a sense of Oneness with the entire universe.

In daily Dahnhak Practice, Un-Ki-Shim-Gong follows the Hang-Gong exercise. Like Hang-Gong, Un-Ki-Shim-Gong is composed of nine levels. Practitioners understand how to control the movement of Ki-energy through the power of concentration.

Un-Ki-Shim-Gong Level 9

Posture: Sit in a half lotus posture with the spine straight and the hands on the knees. Bring the hands in front of the navel with palms facing but not touching. Slowly move the hands apart and then back to within a couple of inches of each other.

Practice: Begin by simply moving the hands back and forth in front of the navel. After this becomes natural, combine the hand movements with breathing. While inhaling, pull the hands apart. On exhaling, bring the hands together, but not touching.

Un-Ki-Shim-Gong Level 8

Posture: Sit in a half lotus posture with the spine straight and the hands on the knees. Bring the left hand to a position in front of the Lower Dahn-Jon with the palm facing up and the little finger touching the Dahn-Jon. Place the right hand at chest level with the palm facing downward.

Practice: With hands in these positions, slowly raise

the right hand up to the level of the In-Dang(the acupressure point between the eyebrows). Gently lower the right hand down to within a couple of inches of the left hand. Repeat the movement of the right hand between the In-Dang and the Lower Dahn-Jon several times.

This practice stimulates the 3 major energy centers in front of the body: Upper, Middle, and Lower Dahn-Jon.

Un-Ki-Shim-Gong Level 7

Posture: Sit in a half lotus posture with the spine straight and the hands on the knees, palms up .

Practice: Concentrate on the hands and move the Ki-energy throughout the body to the hands. Let the Ki-energy lift the hands up. Let them move slowly to a position on each side of the head, as if petals were blooming without a sound. Let both hands remain by the side of the head and feel the Ki-energy. Concentrate on the Ki-energy moving through both Jang-Shims, Myong-Mun, and Dahn-Jon.

Dahn-Mu: Flowing with Ki-energy

"Dahn" means "Ki-energy." "Mu" means dance. Dahn-Mu is a form of dancing with the natural flow of Ki-energy.

This gentle dancing is an effective method to control and utilize Ki-energy. Practitioners usually experience Ki-energy as a gentle vibration inside the body. The Ki-energy usually begins in the hands, quickly moves through the whole body until the entire body is responding in dance-like movements, called Dahn-Mu.

This exercise is particularly easy to accomplish since there is nothing to learn in the way of technique. The alignment of the body with Ki-energy is influenced by the state of mind of the participant. The resulting Dahn-Mu might be expressed with fast or slow motions, restrained or passionate movements. The expression of Ki-energy may include complex and intricate movements that a person might not normally make. When the rhythmic flow of Ki-energy is followed with movement, practitioners dance naturally, ignoring the long repressed and inhibited movements that they may have held in the past.

These graceful motions come from deep within a person's being as a perfect, spontaneous expression of the vital energy. Out of these dance-like movements of self-expression, practitioners begin to experience a gentle dynamic meditation from a subconscious state.

As the dancing progresses, practitioners will begin to feel joy and blessings bubbling up from within. Tears may erupt, releasing blocked emotions locked in the chest. Freely crying during the dancing movements is the best way to release old tensions and bring about a sense of peace.

Experiencing Dahn-Mu brings forth a true understanding of freedom. Allowing the spontaneous dancing movements is the same as trusting the benevolent wisdom of cosmic energy. After realizing the way the Ki-energy works, through the dance movements, practitioners can easily gain control and utilize the Ki-energy at will.

Ki-energy has the power of rehabilitation by balancing and harmonizing the flow of Ki-energy through the body. The relationship between the body and Ki-energy provides a source of understanding, accessed through intuition, which tells practitioners how to move the body for the most beneficial healing results. For example, if someone has a pain in the shoulder, Ki-energy may direct him/her to use a circular motion to open the blocked meridian channels.

Dahn-Mu is a self-healing process. It stimulates the energy centers and meridian channels, bringing Ki-energy to the entire body and a feeling of unlimited joy and peace.

Dahn-Mu 12 Forms

"Dahn-Mu 12 Forms" are made with 12 simple, natural motions which express profound philosophical meaning.

The Dahn-Mu 12 Forms open up all acupressure points along the energy meridians for the unobstructed movement of Jin-Ki throughout the body. As these 12 Forms become more familiar, practitioners begin to move in a natural and beautiful manner using the flow of Ki-energy.

1) Arirang Form
This Form is from a Korean traditional folk dance

called "Arirang" which means "the joy of finding one's True Self." Dance walking forward, nodding the head to one side and then the other side while, at the same time, moving the arms up and down as if flying like a bird. The dancer reaches a peaceful and happy state of mind on the way to find the real Self.

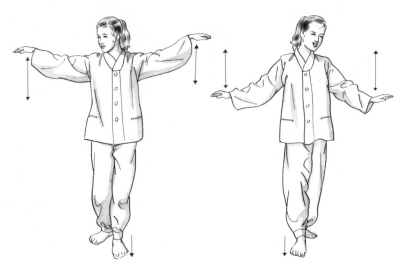

2) Giving and Taking Form

Stepping one step forward, bend over at the waist with a straight back, and move the hands from the chest out in front of the body as if giving out love. Stepping another step, move the hands as if receiving love.

3) Giving All My Love Form

Dance walking forward, moving the hands in a motion as if pouring the love out of the heart to the beloved.

4) Hugging My Beloved Form #1

Dance walking to one side, with arms first out-stretched and then clasped around the shoulders as if hugging a loved one. Repeat this motion with each step. When stepping with the left foot, look to the left. Repeat the motion with the right foot looking to the right.

5) Hugging My Beloved Form #2

Dance walking forward in the same manner as in Dahn-Mu 4.

6) Heaven and Earth Form

Dance walking forward with the right hand raised towards the sky and the left hand lowered to the earth. Continue the forward motion reversing the hand positions. This motion uses the body and arms to connect Heaven and Earth.

7) Sowing Seeds Form

Dance walking forward as if you, as a farmer, were sowing seeds in the field.

8) Touching Heaven Form

Dance walking forward, moving the right arm up from the waist to above the head. Make a circle with the palm as if touching Heaven. Gather up the celestial energy above the head and bring it down into the Lower Dahn-Jon. Repeat the motion with the other hand.

9) Flying Dragon Form

Dance walking forward, moving the hands as if you were a dragon flying up to Heaven wagging its tail.

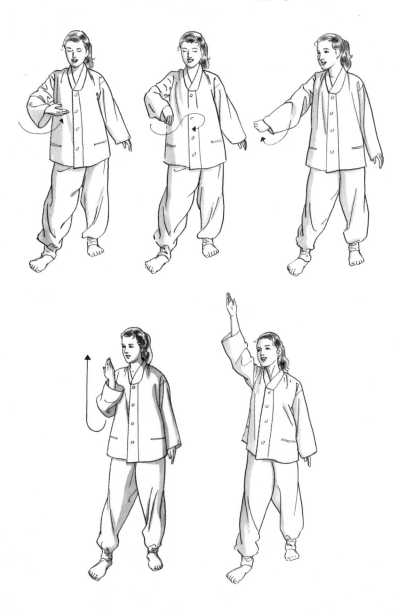

10) Balancing Plate Form

Dance walking forward as if holding a plate on the left palm, rotating it under the left arm and over the head being very careful not to drop it. Repeat the motion with the right hand.

11) Divine Hand Form

Open your arms, walking forward, dance as if you take aim at the ocean with right hand, and divide it with left hand. Repeat the motion with the other side.

12) Tiger Form

Dance while moving the arms in a chopping motion from over the shoulder to one side, like a tiger chopping through mountains and rivers.

Dahn-Gong: Advanced Level of Martial Arts

"Dahn" means Ki-energy. "Gong" means martial arts. Dahn-Gong is the advanced level of martial arts developing from outflow of Ki-energy accumulated through practicing Dahn-Mu.

Through the practice of Dahn-Mu, Ki-energy is stimulated throughout the body. Acupressure points are opened and Ki-energy is freely moving throughout the meridian channels. The body aligns with the universal Ki-energy and accumulates Ki-energy whenever necessary.

Dahn-Gong is the next step for practitioners to improve physical health and increase mental powers. The result of Dahn-Gong practice is the development of a well-rounded disposition based in the harmonious relationship between body and mind, facilitated by the accumulation of Ki-energy.

Through Dahn-Gong practice, practitioners feel the power in the body through the flow of Ki-energy.

Dahn-Gong Forms

Dahn-Gong is comprised of five forms which stimulate different patterns of Ki-energy circulation.

1) **Basic Form**: Corrects the skeletal structure.
2) **Accumulative Form**: Accumulates Ki-energy to increase power in the body and mind.
3) **Girdle Form**: Increases and controls the circulation of Ki-energy through the Lower Dahn-Jon and the Girdle Meridian Channel, Dae-Mak.

4) **Microcosmic Form**: Increases and controls the circulation of Ki-energy through the Conception-Governor Meridian Channel, Im-Doc-Mak.

5) **Macrocosmic Form**: Increases and controls the circulation of Ki-energy through the 12 meridians and 365 acupressure points.

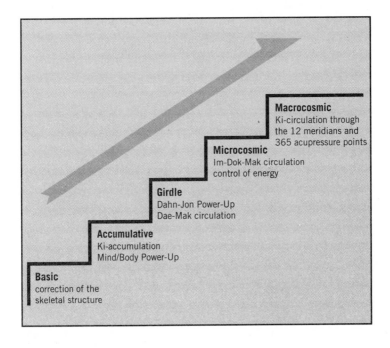

Macrocosmic
Ki-circulation through the 12 meridians and 365 acupressure points

Microcosmic
Im-Dok-Mak circulation control of energy

Girdle
Dahn-Jon Power-Up
Dae-Mak circulation

Accumulative
Ki-accumulation
Mind/Body Power-Up

Basic
correction of the skeletal structure

Basic Dahn-Gong Form

The Basic Dahn-Gong form is composed of 12 movements which are designed to stretch the arms and legs, strengthen the muscles and correct the skeletal structure. Each movement combines a strong, powerful motion to balance the body with a relaxation technique to spread Ki-energy to the entire body.

1) Preparation

Standing with both feet together and hands at the side of the body, move the left leg in a half circle motion until the legs are open shoulder width apart. Raise the arms up to shoulder height with hands in front of chest, shoulder width apart and palms down. Bend the knees slightly and lower the arms.

2) Arms Push Forward

With palms facing forward, bring the hands in front of the armpits. Push the arms forward, extended fully, with palms forward.

3) Open Chest

Bring hands towards chest, but this time cross hands in front of the chest. Bring arms out to the sides, fully extend with palms facing away from the body.

4) Push with a Twist

Keeping legs shoulder width apart, move the left leg back. Twist the body to face to the left. Extend the right arm to the left with the palm facing away from the body and the left hand placed under the right elbow. Change direction of the body, moving the right leg back. Twist the body to the right. Extend the left arm to the right with the palm facing away from the body and the right hand placed under the left elbow.

5) One Hand Push

Twist forward extending the right arm with palm forward in front of the body and left hand at the right elbow. Exchange arms with the left arm extended with palm forward and right hand at left elbow. Let the eyes follow the hand movements.

6) Hand Defense

Move the left leg backward. While bringing in the left hand, move the right hand forward with palm facing to your face as in a defensive posture. Repeat the motion with the left hand.

7) Arm Defense

Stretch the left leg out to the side while bending the right knee. Bend over towards the left foot and stretch the left arm along the left leg towards the ankle with the palm facing down. At the same time, raise right hand with palm facing forward just above the forehead. Repeat the movement for the right side.

8) Open Chest

Cross the arms in front of the chest. Then bring arms out to the sides, fully extended with palms facing away from the body.

9) Open Ah-Mun

Stand with feet wide apart, bring both hands in behind head, crossing the wrists at Ah-Mun. Push each arm out so that the hands are facing in opposite directions with palms out. (The Ah-Mun, a vitally important acupressure point is located between first and second cervical vertebrae.)

10) Upper Body Bend and Twist

With arms extended, bend the upper body forward, looking down. Keep arms extended and twist the arms above the head with palms facing up, and stretch.

11) Holding Up the Sky

Bend the knees and raise the upper body while lowering the arms to the Lower Dahn-Jon. Slowly raise the hands with palms up past the Middle Dahn-Jon, Upper Dahn-Jon and above the head. When the hands reach the

highest point, the wrists twist for the palms to face up, with a shout.

12) Hand Clap above Head

Slowly lower the arms crossing the wrists as they descend to the Lower Dahn-Jon and bring the feet together. Continue the circular movement of the arms out to the side of the body and bring the arms back up above the head. The palms come together with a strong clap of the hands.

13) Completion

With the palms together, exhale slowly, only releasing 80% of the air inside the lungs as the hands lower in front of the body to the Lower Dahn-Jon. Drop hands to the side and exhale the remaining 20% of the breath, lowering the head.

5. Special Dahnhak Training Courses

These courses are summaries of other Dahnhak Training Courses which are available to practitioners. These practices are conducted by a Dahnhak instructor.

Gae-Hyol: Meridian Channel Awakening

"Gae" means "open or awaken." "Hyol" is the name for the acupressure points in human body. This practice opens up the 365 acupressure points, and the 12 meridian channels, restoring the natural flow of Ki-energy throughout the body. When all the blockages are removed, practitioners feel a balance between the body and mind because the Ki-energy is in balance.

After practicing Gae-Hyol, practitioners are able to breathe more deeply. A sense of emotional stability and mental clarity arises out of this practice which facilitates deeper meditation.

Shim-Sung: Developing a Relationship with the Self

"Shim-Sung" means "True Self." This practice helps the practitioners see through the defensive walls of the ego, past controlling dramas, to finally discover their True Self. With this discovery, they uncover their life's purpose.

Practitioners dispense with their old habits, emotions, and fixations. The empowering experience of meeting their True Self instills self-confidence, acceptance and happiness. Knowing the True Self leads to developing harmonious relationships based on trust and love.

With the changes in their personalities through Shim-Sung, practitioners are able to realign their lives towards their true purpose. They can set up the goal of working towards Human Perfection to improve not only their lives but the lives of people around them.

Hwal-Gong: Therapeutic Exercise

Hwal-Gong facilitates the self-healing of the body by activating and maximizing natural healing powers. Practitioners learn to consciously control the Ki-energy flow to heal.

Hwal-Gong is called "giving love" or "mindful caring." It is a unique Dahnhak Practice teaching the principles of accessing loving Ki-energy to help others heal and revitalize their energy. This is an enriching practice because it benefits everyone practitioners come into contact with in the home, workplace or community.

Brain Respiration: Energizing and Rejuvenating the Brain

Brain Respiration is a practice which realigns and balances the energy circuits in the brain to return practitioners to an original state of perfection, both physically and mentally.

This is a very easy and simple practice based on recently discovered anatomical facts about the hippocampus. The hippocampus is the part of the brain that controls human emotions. Human emotions arise out of memories stored in the hippocampus. With the purification of the hippocampus, many emotional problems can be resolved. This is a new approach to dealing with complicated mental problems which have been difficult to mediate in the past. Through Brain Respiration, practitioners can change the physical structure and the energy system in the brain with surprising results. Mental capabilities increase including access to cosmic wisdom and ancient truths. Brain Respiration opens up the unlimited potential of the human mind.

Taorobics: Combining Tao & Aerobics

Taorobics is the spontaneous bodily expression of the Oneness of human energy and cosmic energy. The basic movements of Taorobics utilize a spiral motion to activate the meridian system and reintegrate the functions of bodily organs and mental activities. The movements are so natural that the body moves easily without irritating joints or muscles.

Taorobics is the movement of Ki-energy through the open meridian channels inside the body. The relaxed body dances with the rhythm of the Ki-energy flowing through it. The mind and spirit awaken to a higher dimension of experience and practitioners feel unlimited joy and freedom. It is a joyful way to reach holistic health.

The natural combination of spontaneous motions corrects the spinal structure. When the body is balanced, the individual is energized and revitalized. Taorobics is the gate to the inner Self. A relaxed, peaceful, joyful, positive view of life is accessible. Through Taorobics, the vivid experience of Ki-energy encourages a broader mental perspective, clearer understanding, and greater enjoyment of life.

PART Ⅳ

SHARING

Personal experiences from the Dahnhak practitioners are always beneficial to the beginning student. It encourages practitioners to work through frustrating periods and towards a goal of self-renewal.

More than Recovering Health

Ron Higgins
Flagstaff, Arizona

In the summer of 1997, I became very ill. A few years earlier, I had been diagnosed with ulcerative colitis. Prior to this, I had always been very active and had seen myself as being "healthy." As my condition worsened, it became obvious to me that I had a very big problem. I could no longer ignore the signals that my body was sending to me.

By Christmas, I was having a lot of difficulty functioning at all. I wanted to feel well again, but I didn't know how to reverse the process. My doctor could only offer powerful medications and a deepening, fatalistic resolve of doom and gloom. "It's genetics," he said. "You've been doomed since birth."

I could not accept his opinion and began to search for alternative methods for treating and improving my condition. Little did I know at the time that I was about to begin an incredible journey, which would change my life in ways that reached well beyond my physical well-being.

In January, 1998, after reading several books on healing and natural ways to health, I decided to try acupressure therapy. Searching through the local "Yellow Pages," I found an intriguing sounding place in Sedona called "The Dahn Center." I made an appointment that day and took an hour-long drive for my first session.

The two people that I met there were very friendly, and immediately, I sensed the concern that they felt for my condition. I had never experienced acupressure therapy before. After the session was over, I had no idea why, but I felt well again in a way that I had not felt in a long time. It was at this point that I knew that I was onto something good.

My next visit to the doctor reinforced my feelings about Dahnhak. Even though my doctor had now given up hope, my tests after the treatment were normal. My doctor appeared to be at a loss for an explanation and asked me what I was doing. I explained to him that I had been receiving acupressure treatments and that I was going to meditation classes.

By the summer of 1998, I was feeling much stronger and healthier. My time at the Sedona Dahn Center had a very magical quality about it. But I needed an operation to reduce the affects of my chronic ulcerative colitis. I flew to the Mayo Clinic in Rochester, Minnesota, for surgery. Immediately after surgery, I could feel that my energy had drastically changed. It was as if a poison had been removed from my body. My doctors were astounded by how rapidly I recovered. I was released from the hospital in half the time that had been predicted. Within two weeks, I was taking vigorous walks. Originally, I was told that it would take up to six weeks to recover. Instead, I returned to work 13 days after major surgery. A second operation went as smoothly as the first.

I began this journey searching for help with my disease. And, along the way, I found that I was really searching for myself. In the midst of my suffering, I discovered incredible joy. In Dahnhak, I have had the opportunity to meet people who, through their love and prayers, have pushed me onwards towards self-discovery. At the same time, I have been able to touch many others in a profound way. I never dreamed that this terrible illness would bring me anything but misery and pain. I am no longer in need of any medical treatment and I still practice Dahnhak every day.

Finding My Soul and the Self

Jill Johnson
New York, New York

My work as a Personal Trainer is an intimate experience for my clients as well as for me. It involves sharing what is good and beautiful about life as well as what is good and beautiful about the person with whom I am working. I need to feel physically and mentally up to the task to create beauty and positive feelings in my clients. It is my job to make them feel great about themselves.

Like many other people, I experienced severe depression over the loss of a loved one due to divorce. Here I was, a lover of all sports, a former dancer, a movement expert, paralyzed by depression. I gained fifteen pounds.

My therapist and I decided to try Prosaic because I feared I would lose my clients if I was not able to play the part I knew so well. I experimented with this antidepressant for the recommended six months. I knew in my heart the depression was there for a reason and could not be masked just to make sure I got out of bed every day. The six months came and went and, although I was helped, I was still not moving. A longtime friend and masseur recommended the training at the Dahn Center.

From my first visit five and a half months ago to this day, my progress towards finding my soul and the Self that the depression was pointing to has been remarkable. Added to my weekly schedule were three hours of classes at the Center and an outing to Bear Mountain on Sundays for a short hike. I was reminded of the joy I felt as a dancer. The

Dahnhak classes involve music and movement from the self-expression. Love comes not only from the masters, but from the comfortable surroundings and other students as well. As a group we are taking the responsibility for our well-being, happiness, and health. The three classes per week are structured into three parts. The first part involves simple and straightforward exercise to open the lines of Ki-energy or meridian channels. They are repeatable, easy, safe, and often relaxing exercises. We empty our minds and meditate on the healing Ki-energy. This is the Dahnhak Practice. It is the quieting of the mind to hear one's true calling or voice and the loving atmosphere of trust that helps us reach that place. The hour ends with strength training exercises to continue to do Dahnhak Practice with less exertion and more mental relaxation. It is a glorious, simple practice combining the philosophies of many of the schools of thought I have studied over my 25 year career.

The results from the Dahn practice keep building for me to the point of experiencing genuine happiness and well-being. I smile more, attract more clients, concentrate on clients better, and have the energy to do more for them and for myself. My self-confidence and my ability to understand my behavior and that of others have increased so that I treat myself and others more gently. I have opened my heart to the possibility of loving and being loved again. I have begun to feel the way I felt as a girl, a lighter, more confident sense of myself. While I have gained this sense of emotional well-being, I have lost eight pounds.

Living in a World of Complete Harmony

Laura S. Killian
Phoenix, Arizona

Almost a year ago, I began a long journey; I entered the local Dahn Center with the intent of losing weight. I started Dahnhak Practice on May 18th, 1998. Little did I know the changes in myself that would take place over the next year. When I began the program, I was self-conscious and my low self-esteem caused me to withdraw from the people around me.

When I began doing the daily exercises, I could feel something in me change. I could feel all of the muscles in my body. Through the breathing exercises, I began to feel a big change in my energy level on a daily basis. I also began to enjoy myself at the Center.

I remember one day I came to the Center for class. I walked in and sat down in my usual spot, the far back corner of the room. This time, before the class began, one of the masters smiled at me and asked, "Why don't you move to the front of the classroom?" I must have looked stunned. He encouraged me with his smile and said, "How will you ever gain confidence if you hide in the back of the room?" Well I moved to the front corner and I have been there ever since. That was a big step for me.

I began to experience many things from my daily exercise. I started to feel courage and hope. After a month or so, I also signed up for the special exercises. I started out by taking Gae-Hyol Exercise. I wanted to unblock all the stagnated energy that I had held in my body for so long and restore the free flow of Ki-energy in my body. I also took Shim-Sung, a self-discovery course. The masters said I would learn many things about who I am and why I am the way I am.

I began a weekend course in Shim-Sung as my old Self and at the end I was a totally different person. The course helped me make the changes in myself that I wanted to make. I put 100% effort into the course. I overcame a lot of fears and learned a lot of new things. I realized that my destiny was waiting for me. All I had to do was walk towards it.

I have lost over 40 pounds since I started Dahnhak. My goal was to lose weight but I gained so much more from my experiences. I learned to love myself and everyone around me. I now live in a world of complete harmony and joy.

All My Stress Falls Away

Margrit Hall
San Francisco, California

My name is Margrit. For the past ten months, I have exercised three times a week at the Dahn Center in San Francisco and have advanced to Hang-Gong Level 7. In May, 1999, I found the Dahn Center after thinking about finding a meditation practice for years. I had asked my friends about it and one colleague in particular. In spite of a heavy work load, this person always appeared calm and serene. When I asked him how he was able to stay so composed, he said that he meditated regularly. He then invited me to join him at his meditation class. But I didn't go because it was held on the other side of town. However, I kept thinking about meditation. One day, as I was walking down Geary Street near my house, I saw the sign for the Dahn Center. Without a moment's hesitation, I walked right into the exercise room, which I call, "the blue room."

From the very beginning, I loved Dahnhak Practice. During my first class, I was thrilled to feel the sensation of Ki-energy in my palms. After only a short training period, I learned how to relax my body and mind. It felt so good. As I progressed in my training over the next few months, both at home and at the Center, I felt my body and mind responding to the exercises. During the meditation period of the practice, waves of warmth would sweep through my body, cradling my entire being. From one meditation to the next, I yearned for this experience to return, which it did and continues to do.

At this point, I became more aware of my body. During the exercises, I consciously guided the flow of energy from my hands up to my wrists, arms, shoulders and chest. I imagined opening up my chest; just opening myself up. I felt a strange, wonderful tightness in the middle of my chest responding to my willingness to accept the cosmic energy surrounding me. Since then, I have been nurturing this sensation at the energy point in my chest and conversing with it as if with a friend.

During Gae-Hyol Exercise, I experienced the exhilaration of sharing Ki-energy. Working in pairs and sitting opposite each other, we focused our attention on our hands. Very quickly, in the silence, I felt connected to my partner. I did not know that I had this ability to make a connection with a stranger. I realized that "there is a Sacred Thread that connects us to one another and to our cosmic home."

While the members of the Dahn Center lead their own private lives, when I am in "the blue room," I feel like a member of a family. To me, the Dahn Center is like an island of peace. It's a place where I can return to a loving and lovable Self. Here I am becoming whole again; free and connected at the same time.

The Mind-Body Connection

Katrin Schnabl
New York, New York

I started taking Dahnhak classes regularly in 1995. It was right after my graduation from college. The graduation had been a very stressful and taxing experience. At the peak of all of my activity, I developed major rashes on my skin as an allergic reaction to fibers and chemicals in the processing of fabrics. It scared me, since I had chosen a career in which fabrics were key; fashion design!

Those allergies showed me clearly that something was out of balance, but I didn't have the time or the tools to get to the heart of the matter. Western medicine in the form of cortisone treatments failed to relieve my symptoms.

Because of my health problems, a friend introduced me to the Dahnhak Practice as a way to help me heal myself. As a former dancer, I am used to training my body. I had always been in more or less good physical shape, but often complained about tightness in my lower back and neck. My feet and hip joints were always tight and difficult to loosen up. As a dancer, one is often very critical toward the body's performance. There is some kind of separation between "you" and your tool, the "body."

Both my attitude and my approach have shifted. I am realizing that I can learn about my mind through my body; a lot of information about my mind is hidden or locked in the body. Every thought has a movement and every memory has both a mental and physical place. By training to be more contemplative or listening to myself, I have been able to discover the power of meditation. I have learned the tools to relax myself both physically and mentally through the Dahnhak Practice. My chronic back pain has ceased, and I have improved the flexibility of my joints. But the real difference is the body-mind connection, which I am experiencing for the first time now! In the process, I have been releasing a lot of fear and pain. I have cried a lot, but those were happy tears. I talked to my friends about my feelings and discovered more compassion than I had expected.

The increased vulnerability has opened my heart. I discovered many mental blocks that I had built up long ago as a result of emotional fear and pain. I am learning to be more tender and forgiving to myself, too.

The effect of training is so profound and it is not so easy to explain in words. But it helped me steer through a difficult period of changes and adjustments, providing me with the necessary calm to focus on the task at hand. I moved to a beautiful new home, by myself, found a fulfilling new job, and am currently working on my emotional attachments and expectations. I feel very positive about the future as I have found spiritual guidance.

Newer and Deeper Meaning of Life

Margaret Cazedessus
Sedona, Arizona

Looking back over the fifty-seven years of my life, I have played many roles; daughter, sister, wife, mother, grandmother, friend, associate, teacher and artist. All were fostered with a deep love for life, strong emotion, and a desire for knowledge of greater truths and understanding.

My journey into self-discovery began so long ago. My path would at times be fairly smooth, then, I would experience sudden jerks or surprises. One time, I was diagnosed with a terminal illness. My mind, in a state of shock, began to believe that my choices and lack of understanding had somehow created my condition. I took long serious looks at my life, my responses to life as I understood it, my thoughts I had built up as an evaluation, my choices, my reactions, various situations left undone, individuals who participated and the true desires of my being whether fulfilled or unfulfilled. My mind was deeply moved by my observations. My physical state was stirred to new depths and my emotions were stimulated to new perspectives and ways of expression. My whole being made major shifts as I expanded and healed.

Another trauma arrived which challenged my core. This time it was on the level of the spirit of my being. The spirit I had recognized in my own life when my life was good appeared to be always available to my friends at the Dahn Center. I joined the Dahn Center to experience for myself the clarity and joy my friends were showing.

Almost immediately, I noticed the difference in my out-look. I learned that I am not my body. Instead, my body is mine to use for discovery, clearing, opening and freeing the energy of my mind. We practiced breathing, stretching, holding postures, energy dancing. Never did I tire of the routine as I challenged my body to let go and allow my aliveness. I now know why they all smile at the Dahn Center. They have the true knowledge of who they are and their real purpose in being here. The smile is a natural phenomenon. Smile and the world smiles back... It's wonderful.

My life has taken on new and deeper meaning in a more consistent manner. I am learning to master my own emotions and thoughts. I am freer, more spontaneous and happier. With Dahnhak and its teachings, I have found a beautiful sense of community expressed daily.

True Happiness Inside Me

Lucas Blake
Flagstaff, Arizona

My name is Lucas Blake. I'm 23 years old and a student at Northern Arizona University in Flagstaff, Arizona studying English and Creative Writing. Below is my experience with Dahnhak.

Throughout the beginning of college, I was suffering from very low self-esteem and manic depression. I smoked and drank too much. I was unhappy and unsatisfied. The only thing that I did to make me feel better was write poetry. I tried to teach myself to meditate.

I wanted to become healthier in mind and body, but the regular fitness programs didn't interest me. I wanted to build my self-confidence so I would be more comfortable reading my poetry in public.

I returned to college and started taking martial arts. I was studying Hapkido, a Korean self-defense program, which focused on controlling Ki-energy flow through movement. I was amazed at how I changed after I discovered this kind of energy. I found that I was less interested in learning self-defense, and more interested in understanding the energy. The program helped me learn to relax.

Months later, I found out about a free workshop at the Dahn Center. I was always curious about what happened in there but never had the courage to try it. I went to the workshop and that decision changed my life forever. It was exactly what I was looking for. I found a way to learn about Ki-energy and recover the health of my mind, body and spirit.

As I practiced more, I began to feel the rewards. I developed better endurance through the improvement of concentration. I began to feel true satisfaction in my life by only taking the time to breathe. I began to see the reasons for my depression, loneliness, and low self-confidence. My poetry began to improve, as did my performance in school. I finally found the energy to quit smoking and was amazed at how easy it was. I was able to truly express myself while reading my poetry, and I became very confident and positive in my relationships with other people. I found a source of true happiness inside me, and the more I practiced Dahnhak, the more this source was cultivated.

Dahnhak has helped me in my life in so many ways. I can finally enjoy school and people. I can finally love myself because I have found a way to release all of my fears and anxieties and bring in peace and joy. I have learned that everything I'm feeling is Ki-energy, and everyone feels it. If we learn about this and let go of our old, negative feelings, this entire world can be happy.

In Harmony with Myself and the Universe

Shanan Estreicher
New York, New York

I am a 19 year-old music composer and singer. This is my experience with Dahnhak Practice. Since I was 12 years old, I have had bad digestive problems as well as many other physical ailments. After going to western doctors, an herbalist and naturopathic doctor, I was about to give up. I, then, decided to try acupuncture even though I knew nothing about it. After a few sessions, I started feeling better. I was incredibly happy to see the changes in my body but soon realized that I'd only feel better for a few days, and soon, the problems would return.

After doing some research into the theory behind acupuncture, I learned that the doctor was moving my stagnant energy with the needles. I learned that there were ways in which a person could move their own energy through meditation and martial arts. I was introduced to the Dahn Center by a martial arts instructor. After just a few classes, I saw changes in my body that were much more powerful than I had experienced from the acupuncture.

The changes in my body occurred because of the exercises and meditations that I did in class and on my own. The greatest part is that I started to experience a much calmer mind. This enabled my spirituality to grow as well as my physical body to heal. I began to see the great power of Dahnhak Practice and I began to love it. It has been one of the most important things in my life.

I have been going to Dahn Center for about six

months. I am starting to feel childlike, energetic, confident, lovable, loving, healthy and trusting. This is so much more than I ever thought I'd experience from any training I would recommend Dahnhak Practice to anyone. The exercise balances the whole person so that I become in harmony with myself and the universe. I would like to tell anyone who is beginning the exercise, "Trust yourself and the world around you." It is this trust that enables the greatest work to be done.

HEALTH TIPS

The following exercises will assist practitioners in relieving specific health problems addressed below:

High Blood Pressure

1) Lie down on the back, lift arms and legs straight up from the body, perpendicular to the floor. Shake the arms and legs quickly so that the vibration reaches the whole body. Do this exercise about 1 to 2 minutes once a day.

2) With the fingertips, comb through the hair and stimulate the scalp.

3) Massage, pat, and press the soles of the feet as many times a day as possible. Walk at least once a day for 20 minutes.

Diabetes

1) Sit on the floor with the legs straight and feet together. Move the toes towards the floor, keeping the heels together until the sides of the feet touch the floor. Return the feet to the original position. Repeat this motion rapidly 200 times.

2) With the thumbs, slightly press the two indented portions at the back of the head where it meets the neck. Do this about 5 times.

3) With the thumbs, press the Jok-Sam-Ri 5 times. Follow with hitting the area on the outside of the leg just below the knee with the fists. Finish the exercise by rubbing the area.

Jok-Sam-Ri

Kidney Disease

1) Rub the palms together to create heat at both Jang-Shims. Gently pat the kidneys with the palms. Place the palms on the kidneys, to send Ki-energy into them from the Jang-Shim.

2) Gently press the Yong-Chon on both feet with the thumbs.

3) Sit on the floor with legs stretched out together. Grasp the toes or knees. Exhale and bend the upper torso toward the legs. Rock gently at first, then with additional bounces bend deeper and deeper towards the knees.

4) Gently press the Bak-Ri, located on the back of the leg at the top of the calf. Stimulation of this acupressure point increases the blood circulation to the internal organs, including the kidneys.

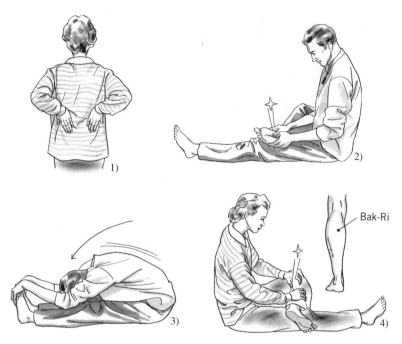

Bak-Ri

Insomina

1) Lie down on the floor with the legs straight and the feet together. Move the toes towards the floor, keeping the heels together until the sides of the feet are touching the floor. Return the feet to the original position. Repeat this motion rapidly 200 times.

2) Lie down on the back and lift the legs into the air. Hit the hips with the heels of the feet.

3) Sit on the floor with the legs about 45 degrees apart. Clasp the toes with the hands. Twist both ankles clockwise and counterclockwise several times.

WHERE TO EXPERIENCE DAHNHAK

Sedona Dahn Institute

3500 Bill Gray Road
Sedona, AZ 86336
USA
Mailing: P. O. Box 2283
Sedona, AZ 86339
USA
800-875-2256, 520-282-4300

CGI Holistic Fitness Center

111 Hormans Ave.
Closter, NJ 07624
USA
201-784-5575

Dahn Centers in U.S.A.

Arizona

Flagstaff Dahn Center
11. S. Beaver St. #3

Flagstaff, AZ 86001
520-226-8381

Phoenix Dahn Center
1404 W. Southern Ave. Suite
E-1
Mesa, AZ 85202
602-464-9068/0348

Sedona Dahn Center
1615 W. Hwy 89A
Sedona, AZ 86336
520-282-3600

California

Fullerton Dahn Center
5931 Beach Blvd.
Buena Park, CA 90621
714-994-1306

Glendale Dahn Center
730 S. Central Ave. #218
Glendale, CA 91204

Irvine Dahn Center
4940 Irvine St.#109 Irvine
CA 92620

Oakland Dahn Center
4000 Broadway #2
Oakland, CA 94611
510-653-5438

Olympic Dahn Center
3053 W. Olympic Blvd #209
Los Angeles, CA 90006
213-381-3893

Rowland Heights Dahn Center
18759 E. Colima Rd.
Rowland Heights, CA 91748
626-912-6064

San Francisco Dahn Center
5746 Geary Blvd. #B
San Francisco, CA 94121
415-752-0800

San Jose Dahn Center
1082 Kiely Blvd.
Santa Clara, CA 95051
408-241-0228

Colorado

DBA Dahn Center
7400 E. Hampden Ave. Suite 6
Denver CO 80231
303-694-2717

Georgia

Atlanta Dahn Center
2505 Chamblee Tucker Rd.
Suite #207
Chamblee, GA 30341
770-234-9940

Hawaii

Hawaii Dahn Center
1936 S. King St. #203
Honolulu, HI 96826
808-942-0003

Illinois

Chicago Dahn Center
4879 N. Lincoln Ave.
Chicago, IL 60625
773-561-7991

Glenview Dahn Center
2630 Golf Road
Glenview, IL 60025
847-998-1377

Schamburg Dahn Center
1063 N. Salem Dr.
Schamburg, IL 60194
847-882-6980

Massachusetts

Boston Dahn Center
10 A Warren St.
Waltham, MA 02154
781-647-7733

New Mexico

Santa-Fe Dahn Center
1807 2nd St. Unit #34
Santa-Fe, NM 87505
505-820-2211

Maryland

Beltsville Dahn Center
5001 Garrett Ave.
Beltsville, MD 20705
301-595-2056

Ellicott City Dahn Center
10194 Baltimore National
Pike #114
Ellicott City, MD 21042
410-418-4404

Rockville Dahn Center
1065 Rockville Pike Talbott
Center
Rockville, MD 20852
301-545-2991

New Jersey

Northvale Dahn Center

153-55 Paris Ave. 2FL.
Northvale, NJ 07647
201-784-1300

Ridgefield Dahn Center
529 Bergen Blvd. 2FL.
Ridgefield, NJ 07657
201-941-8622

New York

Flushing Dahn Center
136-73 Roosevelt Ave.
Flushing, NY 11354
718-762-6373

Long Island Dahn Center
641 C.E. Old Country Rd.
Plainview, NY 11803
516-822-8575

Manhattan Dahn Center
830 6th Ave. 3FL.
New York, NY 10001
212-725-3262

Woodside Dahn Center
41-07 69th St.
Woodside, NY 11377
718-205-4435

Texas

Houston Dahn Center
1803 Gessner Rd.

Houston, TX 77080
713-464-7012

Virginia

Annandale Dahn Center
6924-C Little River Trunpike
Annandale, VA 22003
703-658-6440

Dahn Centers in Canada

Beaches Dahn Center
2181 Queen St. E. #300
Toronto, Ont., M4E 1E5
416-686-5492

Bloor Dahn Center
617A Bloor St.
W. Toronto, ONT M6G1K8
Canada
416-530-0947

Mississauga Dahn Center
2395 Cawthra Rd. #203
Mississauga, ONT L5A2W8
Canada
905-281-3467

North York Dahn Center
181 Cooksfield Ave. Unit#1
North York, ONT M3H3T4
Canada
416-630-3157

Dahn Centers in England

Exeter Dahn Center
Bellenden Wrefords Lane
Exeter, EX45BR
England, UK
139-249-3491

London Dahn Center
St. Anselm Hous 240
Burlington Rd.
New Malden Surrey KT34NN
England, UK
181-255-4222

Dahn Centers in South America

Asuncion Dahn Center
Tte. Farina 1410 c/Pai Perez
Asuncion, Paraguay
21-213-627

Bom Retiro Dahn Center
Rua Correia de Mello 164
sala 8.
Bom Retiro Sao Paulo-S.P
Brazil SEP: 01123-020
11-230-8280

GLOSSARY

Arirang A Korean traditional folk dance and song, which in Korean means "the joy of finding one's True Self."

Bak-Ri An acupressure point located on the back of the leg at the top of the calf.

Brain Respiration An advanced Dahnhak Practice which realigns and balances the energy circuits in the brain to return practitioners to an original state of perfection, both physically and mentally.

Breath The inhaling and exhaling of air into and out of the body. Breath can either be controlled by the mind or autonomously by the body.

Chon-Ji-Ki-Un Cosmic energy. The Korean word which means highest level of energy.

Chon-Ji-Ma-Um Cosmic mind. The Korean word which means "Enlightened Consciousness."

Dahn-Gong The advanced level of martial arts developing from the outflow of Ki-energy accumulated through practicing Dahn-Mu.

Dahnhak A holistic health program which teaches people how to utilize Ki-energy.

Dahn-Jon An energy center in the body, created by several acupressure points working synergistically, where Ki-energy is accumulated.

Dahn-Jon Breathing A holistic meditative method of respiration to take vital cosmic Ki-energy into the body and accumulate it in the Dahn-Jon. The accumulated Ki-energy increases the natural healing power of the body by strengthening the immune system and supporting the functions of the organs.

Dahn-Jon System The interrelated system of seven Dahn-Jons or energy centers in the body, composed of three Internal Dahn-Jons and four External Dahn-Jons.

Dahn-Mu A form of dancing with the natural flow of Ki-energy, called in Korean "the dance of Ki-energy."

Do-In Exercise A systematic stretching exercise which relieves stiffness and gets the Ki-energy flowing. It helps the mind and body relax before beginning Dahn-Jon Breathing and other Dahnhak exercises.

External Dahn-Jons Energy centers, as part of the Dahn-Jon System, located in the palms of both hands and the soles of both feet.

Gae-Hyol An advanced Dahnhak exercise, which in Korean means "meridian channel awakening," that opens up the 365 acupressure points and the 12 meridian channels, restoring the natural flow of Ki-energy throughout the body.

Hang-Gong A series of nine meditative exercise levels, each level composed of five postures, designed to facilitate deep Dahn-Jon Breathing. Hang-Gong fortifies the meridian system and improves the body's self-healing mechanisms.

Hoe-Um An acupressure point located at the perineum.

Hwal-Gong An advanced Dahnhak Practice, which in Korean means "giving love" or "mindful caring," that teaches practitioners the principle of accessing loving Ki-energy to help other people heal and revitalize their energy.

In-Dang An acupressure point, located between the eyebrows which is called "the eye of Heaven" or "the Third Eye."

Internal Dahn-Jons Energy centers, as part of the Dahn-Jon System, located in the abdomen, chest and between the eyebrows.

In-Hyong Meridian exercises which make up the Human Form section of the Do-In Exercise in which all the exercises encourage the development of harmonious relationships between partners.

Jang-Shim An External Dahn-Jon, part of the Dahn-Jon System, located at the center of the palm on each hand.

Je-Jung An acupressure point located at the navel.

Ji-Gam Exercise A meditative exercise, which means in Korean "detaching from outer consciousness of the five senses and going into the inner consciousness of the sixth sense," to introduce the awareness of Ki-energy through direct experience.

Jin-Dong A healing phenomena that occur when the body begins to shake because either (1) a sufficient accumulation of energy is reached and is beginning to flow rapidly through the meridian system, or (2) there is an influx of vital cosmic energy occurring after fully opening the mind by moving into a deeply relaxed, alpha brain wave state.

Jin-Ki Unlimited Ki-energy which is received through pure cosmic awareness and accessed through deep mindful concentration of the breath.

Jok-Sam-Ri An acupressure point, located on the outside of the leg, just below the knee, and in-between where the two leg bones meet.

Jong-Chung, Ki-Jang, Shin-Myong One of the three principles of Dahnhak Practice, which means in Korean "health to enlightenment," referring to specific steps that people take when they move towards enlightenment.

Jon-Jung An acupressure point between the breasts.

Jong-Ki Limited Ki-energy which is acquired from outside nourishment, such as diet and respiration.

Ki-energy The cosmic vitality or cosmic energy which circulates throughout the universe and is the true essence of every creation in the cosmos.

Ki-Hae An acupressure point, located about 2 inches below the navel, which means "the sea of Ki-energy."

Kyong-Hyol The Korean word for the acupressure points in the body through which Ki-energy enters the body.

Kyong-Rak The Korean word for the meridian channels through which Ki-energy moves throughout the body.

Lower Dahn-Jon An energy center, part of the Dahn-Jon System, located two inches below the navel and two inches inside the abdomen. The Lower Dahn-Jon accumulates Ki-energy and circulates the energy throughout the entire body.

Meridian System The pathway of Ki-energy through the body.

Middle Dahn-Jon An energy center, part of the Dahn-Jon System, located around the Jon-Jung, an acupressure point between the breasts. When Middle Dahn-Jon is activated, practitioners feel peaceful and have the capacity to direct unconditional love towards others.

Myong-Hyon A healing phenomena when cold-like symptoms develop and the body feels tired, weak or heavy. When this occurs, the Ki-energy is washing out toxins held by stagnant energy in the body.

Myong-Mun An acupressure point, located on the back opposite the navel between the 2nd and the 3rd lumbar vertebrae. In Korean, it means "the gate of life" and is the point through which the vital cosmic Ki-energy flows into the body.

Shim-Ki-Hyol-Jong One of the three principles of Dahnhak Practice which means in Korean, "from mind to matter," referring to the understanding of how material existence, including the universe, came into being and the direction all matter is ultimately becoming.

Su-Seung-Hwa-Kang One of the three principles of Dahnhak Practice which means in Korean, "water energy up, fire energy down," which is a universal principle for both nature and the human body.

Shim-Sung An advanced Dahnhak Practice, which in Korean, means "True Self," that uncovers the ego, past controlling dramas, leading one to discover the True Self.

Tae-Chung An acupressure point, located on the top of each foot, at the point where the bones of the big toe and second toe join, between the first and second metatarsal.

Taorobics The spontaneous bodily expression of the Oneness of human energy and cosmic energy. Taorobics utilizes spiral motions to activate the meridian system and integrate the functions of bodily organs and mental activities.

True Self That part of an individual which is in touch with the higher aspects of being human.

Un-Ki-Shim-Gong An exercise which focuses on extremely slow and relaxed movements of the arms and hands called "the motionless-motion." In Korean, it means "the art of circulating Ki-energy with the power of mind or consciousness."

Upper Dahn-Jon An energy center, part of the Dahn-Jon System, located near the In-Dang, an acupressure point between the eyebrows. When it is activated by pure energy, it provides an experience of clear awareness.

Won-Ki Limited Ki-energy which is inherited through genetic information from the parents.

Yong-Chon An External Dahn-Jon, part of the Dahn-Jon System, located on the sole of each foot. It is approximately in the center of the foot and just below the ball.

INDEX

Acupressure points - 36, 40
  Bak-Hoe - 41
  Hoe-Um - 42
  In-Dang - 41
  Myong-Mun - 42
  Jang-Shim - 42
  Je-Jung - 56
  Jok-Sam-Ri - 42
  Jon-Jung - 41
  Ki-Hae - 41
  Tae-Chung - 42
  Yong-Chon - 42
Bak-Hoe - 56
Brain Respiration - 139~140, 173
Breath - 34~35
  Relationship with Ki-energy - 34
Chon-Ji-Ki-Un - 64, 173
Chon-Ji-Ma-Um - 65, 173
Dahn-Gong - 70, 126~137, 173
  Basic Form - 126
Dahnhak - 26~141
  Definition - 25
  Exercises - 74~138
    Body Patting - 44~45

Dahn-Gong - 126~137
Dahn-Jon Breathing - 55
Dahn-Jon Stimulation - 51
Dahn-Mu - 114~125
Do-In - 74~96
Hang-Gong - 100~109
Intestine - 48
Ji-Gam - 97~99
Un-Ki-Shim-Gong - 110~113
History of - 26
Personal Experiences - 145~161
Principles of - 46
Purpose of - 27
Steps of - 69~71
  Initiating - 69
  Accumulating - 69
  Controlling - 70
  Commanding - 70
  Completing - 71
Training Courses - 138~141
  Brain Respiration - 139
  Gae-Hyol - 138
  Shim-Sung - 138
  Hwal-Gong - 139

Taorobics - 140

Dahn-Jon - 55~60

  Breathing - 55

  Exercises - 55

    Breathing Exercise of Accumulating Ki-energy - 55~56

    Hang-Gong - 100~109

    Positions for - 59~60

  Lower - 37~38

  Middle - 37~38

  Upper - 37~38

Dahn-Jon System - 36~39

  External - 39

  Internal - 37~38

Dahn-Mu - 114~125

  12 Forms - 115~125

Diabetes - 164

Do-In Exercise - 74~96

  Chon-Hyong (Heaven Form) - 75~83

  In-Hyong (Human Form) - 83~90

  Ji-Hyong (Earth Form) - 91~96

Energy Circulation - 38, 61

Exercises - 74~137

  Body Patting - 44~45

  Dahn-Gong: Advanced Level of Martial Arts - 126~137

  Dahn-Jon Breathing - 55

  Dahn-Jon Stimulation - 51

  Dahn-Mu: Flowing with Ki-energy - 114~125

  Do-In: Meridian Exercise - 74~96

  Hang-Gong: Dahn-Jon Breathing Postures - 100~109

  Intestine - 48

  Ji-Gam: Ki-energy Awareness - 97~99

  Un-Ki-Shim-Gong: Conscious Control of Ki-energy - 110~113

Gae-Hyol - 138

Hang-Gong - 100~109

  Level 7 - 107~109

  Level 8 - 103~106

  Level 9 - 100~103

Headaches - 76, 81

Health Tips for - 163~167

  Diabetes - 164

  High Blood Pressure - 163

  Insomnia - 166

  Kidney Disease - 165

Health to Enlightenment - 52~53

High Blood Pressure - 163

Hoe-Um - 41, 175

Hwal-Gong - 139

In-Dang - 38, 112, 175

Insomnia - 166

Intestines - 48~51, 54, 59, 76

  Constipation - 48~49

  Intestine Exercise - 49, 51, 57

  Intestinal Problems - 48

Jang-Shim - 37, 39, 103

Je-Jung - 176
Ji-Gam - 69, 97
Jin-Dong - 61~62
Jin-Ki - 33~34
Jok-Sam-Ri - 80, 164
Jong-Chung, Ki-Jang, Shin-Myong - 52~53
Jon-Jung - 38
Jong-Ki - 32~33
Ki-energy - 31~33, 36
    Definition - 32
    Circulation - 27, 38, 110, 126
    Highest Level of - 64~65
    Types of - 32~33
        Won-Ki - 33
        Jong-Ki - 33
        Jin-Ki - 33
Ki-Hae - 42, 50, 56, 59~60
Kidney Disease - 165
Kyong-Hyol - 40
Kyong-Rak - 40
Lower Dahn-Jon - 37~38, 42, 59
Martial Arts - 126~137
Meridian System - 40, 44, 75, 100

Middle Dahn-Jon - 37~38, 52. 70
Mind to Matter - 46, 53
Myong-Hyon - 62~63
Myong-Mun - 56~59
Seung-Heun Lee - 26, 185
Shim-Ki-Hyol-Jong - 46, 53
Signs of Healing - 61~63
Su-Seung-Hwa-Kang - 46~49
Shim-Sung - 138~139, 151
Tae-Chung - 43, 178
Taorobics - 140~141
True Self - 25, 71, 116, 138
    Shim-Sung - 138~139
Un-Ki-Shim-Gong - 110~113
    Level 7 - 112
    Level 8 - 111~112
    Level 9 - 111~113
Upper Dahn-Jon
    - 37~38, 70, 134
Water Energy Up/Fire Energy Down
    - 46
Won-Ki - 32~33
Yong-Chon - 37, 39, 103

ABOUT THE AUTHOR

 **Seung-Heun Lee,** the founder of Dahnhak, having great concern about the state of public wellness, majored in public health and physical education. His zeal and sincerity led him to invest years in research and self-discipline. After much time of devoted effort, he came to a total realization and a comprehensive understanding of the basic principles of life, which he found buried in an ancient Korean traditional wisdom. He rediscovered and modernized the ancient wisdom into a system of holistic health programs which he calls Dahnhak.

Since he opened the first Dahn Center in 1985, he has trained over 1,000 Dahnhak masters. Today, a great number of volunteer teachers offer free daily classes in 2,000 South Korean public parks, and the Dahnhak masters teach over 100,000 people at 360 Centers throughout the world. Dahnhak Practice has won public recognition as a successful and socially responsible program.

Seung-Heun Lee, known to his students as Grand Master Lee, came to the United States in 1994 to share the benefits of Dahnhak Practice with more people in the world. He has been active as an alternative medicine authority, a Ki-Gong master who leads people to the practical experience of Ki-energy, a teacher of educational philosophy and a writer. He has led an active life, helping people to improve their mental and physical health through the various programs of Dahnhak Practice.

In 1997, he established the Sedona Dahn Institute, a holistic health and human development institution, in Sedona, Arizona. Since then, he has been living in Sedona and designing a number of creative training methods to help people activate their own internal energy, facilitate their self-healing mechanisms and obtain enhanced awareness. These methods include Dahn Method, Taorobics and Brain Respiration among others.